The

Why Your Small Business Is

SOCIAL

Wiping Out with Social Media

WAVE

and How to Fix It

Starr Hall

EP
Entrepreneur.
Press

Ryan Shea, Publisher
Cover design: Beth Hansen-Winter
Composition and production: Eliot House Productions

This publication is designed to provide accurate and authoritative information
in regard to the subject matter covered. It is sold with the understanding that the
publisher is not engaged in rendering legal, accounting, or other professional services. If legal advice or other expert assistance is required, the services of a compe-
tent professional person should be sought.

Library of Congress Cataloging-in-Publication Data
Hall, Starr.
      The social wave: why your small business is wiping out with social media
and how to fix it/by Starr Hall.
      p. cm.
      ISBN-13: 978-1-59918-423-4
      ISBN-10: 1-59918-423-0 (alk. paper)
      1. Internet marketing. 2. Social media—Economic aspects. 3. Small busi-
ness marketing. 4. Online social networks—Economic aspects. I. Title.
HF5415.1265.H352 2011
658.8'72—dc23   2011016126

Printed in the United States of America

15 14 13 12   10 9 8 7 6 5 4 3 2 1

CONTENTS

3
BE THE BIG FISH

step-by-step strategies on how to make your brand

4
STOP PADDLING UPSTREAM, START SAILING

how to set up social marketing systems, including

5
KNOW THE TIDE

find out where your customers are posting online and use

6

HOW TO DEAL WITH THE SHARKS ONLINE

7

JUMPING ON THE BLOGGING BOAT

8

THE OCTOPUS APPROACH FOR
VIDEO CREATION AND MARKETING

9
SWIMMING IN A SEA OF CONTENT

10
GET OFF OF THE ISLAND

11
HOW TO CONVERT SMALL FISH INTO BIG FISH

12
THE TIDAL WAVE APPROACH

13
ANCHORING ONLINE RELATIONSHIPS

14
CHECKING OUT SOCIAL SHIPS ONLINE

15
ONLINE HIDDEN TREASURES

16
CUSTOMIZE YOUR SOCIAL SHIP

17
NAVIGATING THE SOCIAL OCEAN

18
MAKE SOME WAVES IN YOUR INDUSTRY

19
VICTORIES AND SHIPWRECKS

FOREWORD BY MICHAEL PORT

I have a young child and every once in a while I'm forced to endure a few hours of video game noise, irritating music, screaming children, frazzled parents, and an unsympathetic adolescent staff at the local Chuck-E-Cheese. When I'm there, however, I secretly enjoy playing the Whack-A-Mole game. You know, the one where you whack the moles but it's never enough because another one always pops up. Well, that's how I feel about the thousands of new, self-proclaimed, "social media experts." It seems like, wherever I turn, another one has popped up.

The current form of social media is really only about five years young. How then, can you have so many people, so expert, at something so new? You might have people who understand how the tools work and can speak the language of social media but, to be a true expert, you need years and years of experience in marketing, PR, and social media. There are really only a few of those types of experts. Starr Hall is one of them.

The mistake many "experts" seem to make with social media is that they get so busy with the trees (tools like Twitter, Facebook, etc.) that they forget the forest (the way all the tools should work together to create a successful, big-picture strategy). The same is true for many books about social media. Countless authors approach social media piecemeal—a book on Twitter or a book on Facebook.

It's easy to break something down, as I've done here. It's harder to build something better in its place. Starr Hall, however, has done it. In fact, I think she's written the perfect book on social media marketing because she's approached the subject from a holistic perspective. Her book will help you create a big-picture strategy for your social marketing and understand the exact tools you need to make it work as well as how to use them.

While reading the book, I heard myself saying, "wow" again and again. I was continuously surprised at how many social media questions, issues, and concerns Starr addresses. Looking back over the book, hard as I tried, I couldn't find a tactic, strategy, or concept missing. Literally, this book covers everything you need to know about social media marketing.

Of course, just thinking about starting what seems to be the uphill trek of social media marketing can tie knots in your stomach and glue your feet to the floor. I totally get it. But it doesn't have to be overwhelming or intimidating. Social media, at its core, is about being social. That you can do. You've been connecting emotionally, intellectually, and spiritually with other people all of your life. Now you just need to do it consciously, using technology as nothing more than a platform. If you do so, with greater awareness and a strategy to boot, it will naturally become as comfortable as a day at the beach—with your laptop, that is.

The first step is to change your perspective on networking. Typical (and traditional) networking conjures up nightmares of the old-school business mentality of scarcity and fear that asks:

- How can I push my agenda?
- How can I get or keep the attention on myself?
- What can I say to really impress or manipulate?
- How can I use each contact to get what I want or need?
- How can I crush the competition?
- How can I dominate the marketplace?

The modern social media strategy should be filled with generosity and grace and ask:

- How can I start and continue friendly conversations?
- How can I put others at ease?
- How can I best express my sincerity and generosity?
- How can I listen attentively so as to recognize the needs and desires of others?
- What can I give and offer to others?
- How can I help others to be successful?
- How can I provide true value to others?
- How can I fully express myself so I can make genuine connections with others?

Furthermore, when we use the word networking, let's think of connecting, instead. Does that help you fall in love with the concept of networking? We don't get contacts, we don't find contacts, we don't have contacts; we make connections with people.

Your networking and ultimately, business success, is determined by other people and how they respond to you. If you keep asking yourself the preceding value-added questions, you'll create a large and powerful network built on compassion, trust, and integrity, a network that is priceless and will reap rewards for years to come.

Oscar Wilde, once said, "Some cause happiness wherever they go; others, whenever they go." When being social online, offline, or in line, for that matter, leave a trail of happiness and others will follow you.

Think big,
—Michael Port
New York Times bestselling author of four books
including *Book Yourself Solid*
www.MichaelPort.com
Twitter: @michaelport.com

PREFACE

It wasn't more than a decade ago when businesses large and small were investing hundreds even thousands of dollars in advertising and paying people a lot of money to write powerful marketing copy for their campaigns. Now businesses are starting to invest not only their money but their time in a new form of marketing...social media. However, most businesses have no idea what they are doing with this new form of marketing, let alone how to make this marketing vehicle work in growing their brand exposure and ultimately drive sales. This book aims to solve these problems and guide you—the business owner, marketing director, brand manager, entrepreneur—in how to utilize quick, easy strategies about online marketing and social media, and how to avoid what just doesn't work. My first book, *Get Connected: The Social Networking Toolkit for Business*, was created to highlight the basics of social networking and online marketing, along with a few get-started strategies to get you better results right away. The emails, posts, feedback, and comments I received have been somewhat overwhelming, so I figured that I had struck a cord with most readers. Therefore, I am back with *The Social Wave*— basically social media and online marketing on steroids, a more intermediate and advanced approach than *Get Connected*. Some of our greatest lessons can come from our attempts and tests. Therefore in this book, I will share my journey, mistakes, suggestions, hair-pulling-out social interactions, successes, and challenges. Basically this is me being transparent: a teacher, friend, mentor, student, and well . . . marketer. I will also share stories from studies, surveys, and a few friends of mine that have been successful online with their efforts. Take what you want and what feels right to you. Although I should say leave the rest behind, I would like to ask that you consider all approaches, suggestions, and resources in this book to help you grow your business and take it to a higher level financially and/or emotionally.

So why me? Why am I writing on social media and online marketing? Well, I didn't just fall into social media and online marketing. I flew into it. More than five years ago, when I decided to sell my public relations agency and travel the globe to present and train business owners on their branding and public relations, I was completely motivated by the social movement. I started to notice a shift in the communications industry when dealing with the media as they were moving to less phone pick-up and more email answering. As I began to move my own communications online, I noticed conversations forming and, more important, how easy it was to contact decision makers, and movers and shakers—and get almost instant media coverage for clients and me. This online world was moving at a speedboat pace, and I wanted to be on board. I was ready. I embraced it. I dug into it. I learned all I could and continued to become a part of the conversations more and more every single day.

As I began to move online and get more involved, I met thousands of important people in a matter of months. I noticed very quickly that a lot of people within my center of influence were not embracing this new movement. In fact it was quite the opposite. They were ignoring it, some even running from it at the speed of light. This aroused my curiosity. I could not understand why businesses and entrepreneurs were not embracing this change (or what some people are referring to as a shift), because their consumer sure was! Brand consumers embraced it way before the actual brands, which is why I feel that they have more influence and more of a voice as compared to the businesses that fought it. Why fight exposure?

I came to understand that businesses and entrepreneurs alike were ignoring this new form of communication and marketing because they were either intimidated and didn't know where to start, or they didn't understand the power behind the voices online. Either way, they were soon going to find out what the ROI (risk of ignoring) would be for their business, which is where we are right now as I write this book.

Businesses are now trying to buy a boat, jump in it, and steer it in a thousand different directions with no chart, no compass, no real destination, and more importantly no basic understanding about how this online social ocean even works. Some businesses are throwing thousands, even millions, of dollars at social media and online marketing. When doing this, there is one key point that is missed: money alone cannot buy a space in this place online. A transparent voice, however, can start a movement and become viral, which in turn can build some pretty amazing relationships with a focused market. Hiring people, agencies, or younger-generation family members to be the voice for a brand because they happen to understand the technology in itself is not necessarily a problem. However, when you have no idea what your voice is online and you are not using it to engage with people instead of sales bitching (aka sales pitching), or just talking to be present on a social site, then you are completely missing the point. But don't worry, that is why you have picked up this book: not only to understand using social media as a marketing vehicle but also how to take your brand voice and message and start to make some waves online.

I am going to dig into your branding and image because these are key foundation items a majority of businesses seem to be missing completely. These areas need to be looked at in depth before you even consider boosting your social media and online marketing efforts. And last, but not least, you need to decide who in the heck is going to manage your marketing actions and journey online, as well as what you are budgeting to make this ongoing. From my personal experience in marketing both online and off, or traditional and new, businesses do not allocate a set minimum budget to continually invest in growing their businesses, but they should. I am not talking about a large amount here, my reader friends. I am referring to just committing to some type of budget. Without a growth budget, you are just playing with a hobby or possibly a company that has no long-term plan to stay in business. So, let's dig into what I call the investment of moola part of your marketing, because it needs to be addressed whether you like it or not. I would rather help you get to a place of happiness with marketing investment than be in a place of anxiety and uneasiness. Although I do not want you to put all of your eggs in one basket in regard to your marketing, I do want you to have a seriously big egg set in the social media and online marketing basket, because communication and technology will continue to grow every single day. (Oh wow, as I type this, Apple just came out with a new product. Surprise, surprise!)

I eat, sleep, and drink marketing every single moment of every day, and I have tried, tested, re-angled, tried again, asked, surveyed, and studied to bring you the best, proven marketing and branding strategies that get results. My constant curiosity and what I call "Shiny-Object Syndrome" are driven by my passion to get businesses known around the globe for the betterment of this planet, our health, and our well-being. My goal in this book is to teach you a minimum of five new things that you have not yet tried to expand the growth, exposure, and revenue of your business. Also be on the lookout for "Wipeouts" throughout this book; these are little side notes that will highlight common issues that people have with social media online, followed by a "Wave Tip" on how you can work through the situation or get better results.

Throughout this book, I encourage you to reach out online and ask me any questions, share insights, or just say hello. You can do that by either Tweeting me @starrhall with the hashtag for this book,

WIPEOUT
"I am not getting people to respond to my posts."

WAVE TIP
Change up your postings by asking questions that you need specific feedback on, keep the post less than two sentences.

#socialwavebook, or visit my Facebook page at www.facebook.com/ starrhalldotcom to post a message to me. I will mention the blog site (www.socialwavebook.com) for this book several times as another option for you to reach out and get further support, ideas, and updates. I am looking forward to your thoughts, lessons learned, and feedback on this book, as well.

Are you going to be prepared and embrace the social wave along with your customers and prospects, or are you going to ignore it and hope it goes away? Because you picked up this book and you are still reading my preface, I am assuming that you are an action taker, that you are ready for a change, and that you are ready to make sense of the social media ocean. Let's do this—together—and make marketing magic happen.

1

SAILING THE SOCIAL OCEAN

top strategies on how you can make social media work for your business

> *The way to get started is to quit talking and begin doing.*
> —WALT DISNEY

I have been socially active online for over five years now and been on email for closer to ten. I remember the learning process I went through just to understand email, let alone each social site. When I first started to become social online, I spent months digging into the layers of the online social world because I knew that it had to be done. I had to learn not only because I was curious about these shiny new objects (yes, I have Shiny Object Syndrome) but also because I knew that communication (also known as marketing) was moving online— and fast. Because I was in the communication industry, if I wasn't involved in this movement or at least informed, I would surely be left behind. As much as I wanted to fight it in the beginning by ignoring invites on LinkedIn and throwing my pen at the computer trying to understand exactly what in the heck Twitter was for, I knew in my gut that I eventually would have to embrace it like I embraced the computer so many years ago. (I will leave out the painful computer memories to spare you an extra 40 pages of reading.)

As I made the move online, it all started to make sense and it was feeling really, really good. Why was it feeling so good you might be thinking? No, it wasn't because I gained thousands of new friends overnight; it was because the result I was getting—finding high-level contacts, making sales, and getting media coverage—was blowing my mind. I could hear angels singing as new emails and requests for consulting, speaking engagements, and more information came in. I started to speak to clients, encouraging them, even begging some, to make the move as well.

I found an unusual resistance to social media as a valuable tool in the communication industry for the first few years; looking back now I realize it was mainly because it was unfamiliar territory. There was a feeling this was an unchartered marketing approach with a bunch of hype, and fears based mainly on the dotcom crash in the '90s seemed to justify the widely-held belief that it was only a matter of time before these social, time-wasting chatter sites would follow. As these fears subsided, a new one somehow has crept in. As businesses begin to move forward and become more involved online, there seems to be a common misunderstanding of social media across the board. Social media is actually not really marketing, it is more like a vehicle to get your message out there, whether it be to the masses or a specifically catered to group or public. I'll explain further. But first, let's talk about "the shift." Over the years I have seen a shift in how we market and how we interact. Social media continues to evolve and become a powerful force and way to reach new and existing customers, clients, and markets. One of the biggest problems with this power vehicle is that businesses do not take the time to understand what happened with this shift. Communication changed, and along with it, our consumers. Because there is a lack of understanding on the brand's side, there is a complete disconnect when a brand attempts to go online and "market" socially.

How social media fits into marketing

To explain where social media fits in, there is an old story that illustrates the differences between advertising, promotion, public relations, marketing, sales, and now social media:

> *If the circus comes to town and you paint a sign that says "Circus Coming to Fairground Saturday," that's advertising.*
>
> *If you put a sign on the back of an elephant and walk him into town, that's promotion.*
>
> *If the elephant walks through the mayor's flowerbed, that's publicity.*
>
> *If you can get the mayor to laugh about it, that's public relations.*
>
> *And if you planned the elephant's walk, that's marketing.*
>
> *If the town's citizens go to the circus, you show them the many entertainment booths, explain how much fun they'll have spending money at the booths, answer their questions, and ultimately, have them spend a lot of money at the circus, now, that's sales!*

Where does social media fit into this illustration? Social media is the vehicle to get your message out there. But, it's no elephant; it's your shiny speedboat! How could you have met the mayor and asked him to either participate in the marketing or give permission to use photos? Why he is on LinkedIn, of course. Where were the pictures posted of the elephant walking through the mayor's flowerbed? On Flickr, Facebook, and, yes, even Twitter, my reader friends. You might even do a blog post on the incident.

Furthermore, you can advertise in specific regions and to specific demographics through Facebook advertising and add some keywords into your blog post for better search engine optimization results. (Don't worry, SEO is covered in Chapter 15. No, don't skip ahead just yet; we need to cover a few other things first.) Many other social sites such as Skype (Skype launched a new advertising platform as of March 2011.

http://mashable.com/2011/03/07/skype-ads-this-week/) and LinkedIn are testing and launching new advertising models. These site vehicles are becoming way more niched just for you, so you can have a better target focus when advertising and reaching out to new prospects. They not only have it narrowed down to demographics, they now have psychographics, as well as spending habits and an individual's center of influence.

center of influence: circle of most influential friends. They are the ones that post and interact with you the most, online or off. They might also be considered "connectors" and influential in their community, again both online and off.

An ongoing problem with social media as a vehicle is that most people only test drive it a few times. They then leave it parked at the dock. They might visit the bay a few times to look at it here and there, but they do nothing else with it. They don't even really buy it. They just visit it occasionally to ponder whether they should buy it or not. They might even get in and sit, look around for a few minutes, and then go back to what they were doing. To that add the saying, "If you do what you have always done, you will get what you have always got." made famous by Anthony Robbins, world-renowned motivational guy. You can't just cruise around the bay, either. You need to go into new areas out there in the ocean to find new fish, go explore new territories, because you can't meet new fish in the same circle of friends or in the same area of the ocean (apologies for referring to us as fish, but hey, for the purpose of illustration in this book, we are running with the wave metaphor).

Although we are learning about social media in this book, a main focus is to teach you how to create waves (aka "buzz") using these social vehicles online to build your brand exposure and show you how you can get powerful publicity by jumping into that speedy boat, riding it up and down the blue coastal waters, and getting a ton of people to post and write about your brand journey and message. This in turn will increase your brand exposure and get people back to your site. You will also learn you what you need to do to build mutually beneficial relationships with site visitors and social connections. So in a nutshell, you will be learning how to get more publicity and exposure online by building quality relationships and utilizing some pretty amazing tools to make marketing magic happen.

You see, publicity builds credibility. As marketing author Al Ries says, "Advertising maintains a brand. Once they are at top of mind, publicity builds them." A great story in his and Laura Ries must-read book, *The Fall of Advertising and the Rise of PR*, is the explanation of Red Bull vs. Coca Cola. It demonstrates how Red Bull built its brand to top of mind and created a new category—the energy drink—all through publicity. Coca Cola decided to go up against Red Bull and launch its own energy drink by investing $31 million in advertising. Hmmm . . . do you know what Coca Cola's original energy drink was? Can't remember it, can you? Red Bull still owns the market. Pick up Reis's book to get the details of that story. It clearly demonstrates the power of publicity vs. advertising. One of the main disconnects that I see in brands online is that they try to be Coca Cola, going online and advertising to launch a brand's presence, which totally defeats the purpose. There is no credibility in advertising. It is just a brand talking about itself and tooting its own horn. Publicity gets other people talking about you and tooting that dang horn for you, which is the key to brand building. (Yep, it's the dang horn thing. That is the key!)

> There are dozens of amazing social media-focused experts online that have a large following. Who knows how they get any sleep with all of the posting and engaging that they do? Some people apparently don't need much sleep. Some true experts include Gary Vaynerchuk, Scott Stratten, Guy Kawasaki, Chris Brogan, and Mari Smith.

Using social vehicles as a listening channel

What is even more mind blowing to me about social media is that businesses continue to ignore it hoping that it will go away. Wetpaint/Altimeter, which specializes in online research, released a 2010 study that found companies deeply and widely engaged in social media significantly surpass their peers in both revenue and profit. The study also found the companies with the highest levels of social media activity had sales that grew on average by 18 percent, while those with the least amount of social activity saw their sales decline by 6 percent.

In addition to becoming a part of our marketing musts to increase exposure and profits, social media vehicles have also changed our everyday language, from "Tweet me" and "Tag me," to some more interesting lingo such as "Bump me," or "Send me a wiki." Five years ago, who would have thought we would be asking to bump or tweet each other? No matter what way you choose to look at it, the online world has become the age of information, and because we are all hungry for information and constantly craving more, the information world (IW) is here to stay. This information age is now evolving through fancy new ways of delivery known as "technology." New technologies such as iPads, iPhones, and text and video messaging allow us to have a voice and share it with whomever the heck we want. Because we all want to be heard, whether it is sharing a great experience at a restaurant or hotel, or a not-so-pleasant interaction with your mobile company, people are talking online about you or to you. Are you listening? Furthermore and even more important, are you there to answer?

So many companies, large and small, are not even online yet. They are still struggling with their 1990s brochure of a website instead of taking time to utilize these social vehicles as a listening tool to help grow their brand presence and consumer loyalty. If you Google or Bing search your company's product or service, you will most likely find that somewhere, someone has been talking about you or trying to find you. If for some off-the-wall reason you do not find any conversation about you, then that is another problem in itself.

Fortune Inc., an online news outlet, studied ten major brands online from Zappos to Bank of America to find out which brands had better online customer service. What it reported was very surprising. While Zappos is referred to as one of Twitter's brightest corporate stars, the old-fashioned telephone still won the day when it came to

Zappos's most effective customer service problem-solving method, and this was also true at Delta, Rubbermaid, and the Hyatt. The brand with the most effective customer service portal online and the highest level of support was yet again another surprise—Comcast. Fortune reported, "They seem to have nailed the telephone and live chat, but Twitter solved the customer service problem." For the full study, visit http://bit.ly/gGHTIv.

Your business growth and exposure online are dependent on your level of presence and interaction. It is time for you to choose a vehicle and set up a listening center online. A few excellent sites for implementing a monitoring outlet are Hootsuite.com or Tweetdeck.com. Both have free as well as trial and paid-for options. ObjectiveMarketer.com, mainly focused on the monitoring aspect of your online brand exposure, is definitely the Ferrari of these tools, so check it out, ask for a demo, and be ready to implement it once you have an online presence that requires a more sophisticated tool. ObjectiveMarketer.com offers what are called "Engagement Reports" so you can see who is engaging online using your brand name, product, or service and their level of engagement. It is also a great site for planning and executing, dare we say it, an online "campaign."

Why do we call it a "campaign"? In the dictionary, a campaign means an "attempt to win; attack." But we are not "attempting to win" or setting out to "attack." So right here and now in this very book, let's change it to "a journey." Yep, a social media journey or a marketing journey. Ralph Waldo Emerson once famously said, "Life is a journey, not a destination," and this rings true with marketing. The opportunities that we come across along the way, the people we meet, the more exposure that we get, the more media coverage—these are all a part

List hours that you are available to chat online, or have live interactive video broadcasts on set days at set times through sites such as Ustream. tv or TalkFusion.com. Then your customers, clients, and prospects can jump on live to ask you questions about your industry, product, or service and interact/ see you on camera, live in person.

of a journey, not necessarily a destination and certainly not a flipping campaign.

Consistency with your online approach

Lack of consistency with a brand message online is something that I must address here. Some brands fail before they really even get started online due to the fact that they are not consistent with when and how they post and interact online. Thus they might post or comment once a week, or what I call "WTFLI" (pronounced *wit-fly*), meaning when they feel like it, which might even be less than once a week. When you do this as a brand, you are basically saying, "I am not listening to what you have to say, nor am I here for you." How would that feel on the prospect or customer's end? It would be like walking into a chamber mixer event for ten minutes with your hands over your ears. You might be able to see people, but you can't hear what they are saying to you, about you, or with you.

There is one very simple way to solve this problem. You need to set a certain time every day when you will go online to answer questions and post. This way there is a consistency as to when you are online, and your connections will begin to communicate with you during those times. Even if they post to you when you are not online, they will at least be informed and know what to expect about when you will be online to answer. I suggest that you have outlets available on sites such as Twitter or Facebook, but that you also create a customer service portal on your website as well.

I will cover more about setting up a customer service portal in a later chapter, but for now just a few basics:

- Incorporate your Twitter and Facebook feeds into a customer service section on your site so they are all in one place. One of the main focuses of your online journey should be to get people back to your site so ultimately they will read more about you and take their relationship with you to a deeper level. You need to make sure that there is an auto-trust component to your site once they land. (I will cover this in a later chapter.) For now, start by being more consistent when you go online and when you answer and interact.

- If you do not want to set a certain time each day, then at least communicate that to your connections and prospects by telling them how you work online and what your availability is.

Another online social offense occurs when brands focus on something completely different every time they post, something that has nothing to do with their core brand message or personality. This can confuse prospects and can be even more upsetting with current customers and clients who already thought they understood your brand message. I am not saying that you need to post the same message all of the time, every day, on the same topic. I am referring to staying in line with your brand personality and what your core brand values and message are all about.

For example, if your brand is humorous and playful, then it would make sense for you to post a funny cartoon about your industry or something funny about one of your team members. Of course, get the team member's permission before you start poking fun at him or around him. If you are this playful brand, posting serious studies and analytics on your industry gives a mixed message. You can certainly post serious statistics about your industry, don't get me wrong. Just make sure that you are playful with it. You could use wording such as "Are they serious

You can set posts online for a later date and time using auto-posting features on social media dashboards such as Hootsuite.com. If you do this, make sure that you are transparent. Let people know that you set the post. For example: I am traveling this week so I set this post on auto because I just wanted you to see this amazing resource, tool, etc. This keeps you active on the newsfeed, communicating with your connections, and the transparency is golden.

about this?" or "Our take is that these numbers suck. How can we improve them?" Again, just add playful to your posts if that is your brand personality and within your core message. In Chapter 3, you will find a brand personality assessment questionnaire that you can fill out to help you better determine what this should be online for your brand.

Leave out the sales bitching

Every time I train or present anywhere around the globe and ask the audience members how many of them like to be sales pitched, it never fails that not one person raises her hand. Well, actually one time someone did. I told everyone in the room to go sit by her and sales pitch her their products. She very quickly changed her position. People do not like to be sales pitched (aka "sales bitching"). So why would you do it online? Really, when you look at successful branding online, 99 percent of those companies built their brand without sales bitching, or pushing products. They built relationships and used social vehicles as listening channels and customer service outlets.

Social media is just not as powerful when you are constantly posting product specials or product and service promotions. That would be called advertising. Pushing products online or off is not being social, and it is not a relationship-building approach. You can always have product information and sales pages on your site, but I suggest that you leave the bitching out of your posting on social sites. It takes power away from your brand presence. It has been proven time and again in study after study that building credibility and relationships are the foundational activities needed to create a top-of-mind brand. Trust and credibility must be built first. People will only buy from you at the level they trust you. Period.

It is not about the numbers

At least several times every month, I come across potential clients that are only focused on the numbers. Because the bottom line has to do with numbers, right? Well, my reader friends (I am assuming that we are friends now, because you are still reading this book and I just know that you have already reached out to connect with me online at www. socialwavebook.com, right?), people are not just a number, nor should they be treated like one. The truth is that the more people you know, the less you really know them. How would you manage quality relationships with 100,000 people? I chose not to have a massive outreach on my social sites because I really want to take the time to answer, get to know people, and engage on a sincere level. When you just focus on the numbers, you often lose sight of standards as well as what quality really means to your business in regard to your ideal customer or client. It is all about quality, not quantity.

I could easily have kept my Twitter numbers at 35,000. Years ago when I first starting using Twitter, I used an auto-follow program, which is how I got my numbers up so high. Yes, they were just numbers. However it hit me one day like a ton of bricks (a cheesy saying that my parents use and passed on to their kids, thanks Mom and Dad!) that bigger does not always mean better, especially when it comes to social media connections. Furthermore, when I realized that half of the people following me where either in the porn industry or they were an online coupon outlet, I knew that was not the way I wanted my online presence to be, let alone my connections. So, I deleted them and started to rebuild. Today, as I write this book, I have 3,500 followers. To some, it's nothing, but to me it is everything because I know or have Tweeted to at least 95 percent of my followers, consistently.

While we are on Twitter, let me share another amazing outcome regarding number of followers. There have often been Tweets for a cause or with a sales focus from celebrity Tweeters resulting in next to nothing in results. Celebrity Tweets (or those of any user with a large follower count) might not help increase awareness or sales on social networking sites. It is more important that the interests of the person with the following are in line with those of the person asking for the ReTweet (RT) or forward, or promotion support.

Analyzing a database of over 500 million Tweets, a Stanford study looked at the relation of Twitter follower count to the ability to spread hashtags. Users with large follower counts did not spread as well as those with smaller follower counts (less than 1000 followers). In another study of influence circulation that looks at high influentials and low influentials in 90 million Twitter posts, the authors found "under a wide range of plausible assumptions the most cost-effective performance can be realized using 'ordinary influencers'—individuals who exert average or even less-than-average influence." (For the study, see http://misc. si.umich.edu/media/papers/wsdm333w-bakshy.pdf.)

A Harvard study in 2009, "Do Friends Influence Purchases in a Social Network?," found it was the moderately connected people, not the highly connected, that were the most likely to be influenced by friends' purchases. (For the complete study, see hbs.edu/research/pdf/09-123.pdf.) There are dozens of other studies available online that show it is not about the numbers, it is about the influence and the messaging, as well as the level of connection. The bottom line is you need to achieve tighter engagement with your followers, not just obtain more.

Your image and branding

Before you dive into this book feet first, let's do a quick image and branding check to make sure that your social ship looks like a yacht, not a sinking fishing boat. It never ceases to amaze me how many brands fail before they even start online because their image is completely off. Rather than looking at their brand image as an investment for the long-term growth of their financial well-being, they use clip art to throw their logo together because they want to save a few hundred dollars, and so they short themselves from day one. With that said, first thing is first. Get rid of the clipart logo. There are way too many online brand image specialists that can create powerful award-winning logos. You can name your budget on sites such as guru.com and elance.com. Make sure you clearly communicate that, per Starr Hall, clipart is not to be used!

Aside from your logo, how is your brand name? What is going on there? There are a few things I would ask you to consider when setting your brand name. If you already have an established name, this might prompt you to change it (warning inserted here). Ask yourself: Do I plan on having this company until I say goodbye to this planet? Or would I like to have an exit strategy and sell it? If you plan on eventually getting out of the business you are in and maybe enjoying some leisure family and vacation time, you might want to consider leaving your personal name out of the company name. Why? Because if you go to sell your company, even if it is worth millions, you are taking away from its salability because the image is based on you. Unless you come with the company (which kind of defeats most of the purpose, don't you think?), you need to get your name off the brand. Now, don't get me wrong. You can use your name to build a brand. I do this with my own company as well as with clients. Build your personal reputation and then branch off mini yous under a different name. For example, my company name for my consulting and training is Starr Hall LLC, and I have and continue to build my recognition and exposure in different markets online and off. I have recently decided to open Cuvée, a champagne bar I plan on franchising. It is a division under my Starr Hall LLC. It has a completely different name, one not based on my name. However, I am using my connections and presence to build the fans, followers, and exposure.

As much as I love to encourage creativity when it comes to brand names, do a name explanation check online to see if other people get it. When I launched Cuvée, I asked people if they knew what it meant. Over 100 people responded with yes, 4 with a no. That is a pretty good brand name understanding, so I went with it. In addition, it was simple—one word so the consumer doesn't have to think to much about it. When I first thought of the name it was Cuvée Champagne and Delights Bar, but that was too long. I knew my consumer target would instantly want to shorten it, so I did it for them. Cuvée.

Consumers did the same thing with Oprah. Her show started years ago as *The Oprah Winfrey Show*. Consumers changed it to *The Oprah Show*, then to *Oprah*, finally to *O*. Pretty soon she will just be a symbol. Same rings true with ATT. Do you even know what ATT stands for? Well, consumers didn't want to work hard to remember American Telephone and Telegraph, so they shortened it. Make sense? Keep it short, memorable, and to the point.

Do not be afraid to ask your connections online about your brand name and image and do not stress out over the four people who don't like it. Definitely listen to their reasons, but if you get 100 people that do like it, you are most likely headed in the right direction. I have found a reasonable rate of return in regard to feedback is between 5 to 7 percent. If you are connected to 1,000 people then you should be getting close to 50 to 70 responses. If you are not, then you need to find out why. There could be several reasons why you are getting a low feedback response.

1. You have not kept your brand or you in front of your contacts on a consistent basis,
2. You are making the survey all about you and your brand and not offering them something in exchange for their time, or
3. The people you are connected to are not as active online and you need to reach out to more people that are active online.

LinkedIn groups are an excellent outlet for this type of discussion and research. Just be careful when asking family and friends because they love you and do not want to cause any upset in their relationship with you for the most part (hey, everyone has a pot-stirrer in their family). Always go to people you know will give you honest and worthy feedback. Usually you will find these are people to whom you are not as deeply connected.

One-way vs. two-way messaging

Amazingly, many marketers and entrepreneurs do not understand how they are communicating to their market vs. how they should be.

There is a science behind marketing, not just the emotional piece. The psychology of it all is just awesome, but let me simplify it so you can get on to learning some really super cool, results-oriented social, online, and publicity marketing. First, let's look at talking to your market one way. An example of this would be putting up a billboard or a print ad with your advertising or marketing message for people to read. This ad only reaches or talks one way with the consumer; it does not have an outlet or way for the consumer to talk back to or with the brand. Therefore a relationship does not grow. The consumer does not feel heard, and he moves on. These types of marketing approaches used to work back in the day—the '60s and even through the '90s—because messaging was not as crowded, technology wasn't taking over our planet, and, I have to say it, consumers just weren't as outgoing in wanting to stand up and be heard. Technology has allowed them to have a voice, be heard, and demand attention.

Now, let's look at two-way marketing; some examples are posting a question, or even a marketing message, on a social site and having a comment box or way of entry for your focus audience to reply back and be heard. This type of conversation helps to start a connection and can help nurture it as long as the brand listens and engages back so the reader and audience sincerely feel heard. You see, when a brand posts back to one reader, other people are going to pick up on that and feel encouraged to join in. Then they might like your fan page or visit your website. You can only go up from there—that is, of course, if you follow the juicy stuff in this book ☺.

Some other forms of two-way marketing using media vehicles are text messaging, email, videos—all of which I cover in this book. But before we jump in here head first, stop and ponder how you have been communicating with your customers or clients. How often do you talk with them, let alone your prospects? Do you have someone on staff that can be your two-way message ambassador or can you hire an intern or even a trusted neighbor? Someone trustworthy has got to be the ears for your brand. If you are not, who will be? You need to commit to this, my business friend, or your social marketing efforts are going to be dead in the water. A few things I suggest you do to help move you from one-way to two-way messaging are:

1. *Check all print and one-way ads.* Find an opportunity to add two-way messaging, such as "For the answer to this go to our fan page at . . ." or "For the coupon code, go to our weblog at . . ."

WIPEOUT

I can't seem to convert my connections to actual sales, what can I do to improve this?

WAVE TIP

Besides starting with relationship building, do what is called at-tagging people on social profiles such as Facebook to get their attention and get them back to your site. You put the "@" sign before their name, find them in the drop down menu, then hit enter, type a quick post to them with more information pointing back to your website URL, remembering to leave out the sales bitch. This will go directly on their wall. See the image below.

figure 1.1–"At-tagging" customers targeted for your message

2. *Assign someone to be the daily two-way ambassador for your brand.* Set a goal for her to listen to a minimum of 100 people per day, and have her send you a brief every Friday on how many people she listened to, how many she engaged, and what resulted from the conversations.

3. *On every email you send, video you post, ad you place, appearance you make, and business card or marketing piece you print, you need to add in your social presence.* I am not just talking about adding in the social site's logo icon to show you are online. You need to give them the darn URL. Try to match your social site URL (called vanity URL and covered in this book) as close to your brand/or product name as possible. If you are the brand/or product, then the vanity URL would be your name.

2

CREATING WAVES

top strategies on how you can make social media work for your business

> *The major difference between the big shot and the little shot is the big shot is just a little shot who kept on shooting.*
>
> —ZIG ZIGLAR

With all of the new sites, technology, and people surfacing online daily, it is no longer about just surfing the internet and finding information. It is now about making it. In order to stand out online, you need to have viral or at least forward-worthy content, information, and personality.

The ripple effect

One of the most powerful approaches I have tried, tested, and witnessed in public relations is what I refer to as "the ripple effect." One of my favorite examples of how the ripple effect works is Martha Stewart, because no matter what you think about this woman, she is a brilliant marketer. Her story starts as a homebased catering business. She invites a few important people over for dinner, shows off her cooking and entertainment styling talents, gets a few local papers to write about her, a morning TV show to cover her cooking and entertainment tips, and then rippled out from there. She went regional, eventually gaining national recognition, appearances, and massive exposure. The ripple effect made the Martha Stewart brand, and if you dig deep enough, it is the reason behind the success of most top-of-mind brands around the globe. Ellen DeGeneres, Zappos, Red Bull, documentary movies such as *The Blair Witch Project* and *Fahrenheit 911* all became viral from the ripple effect.

The main point of this approach is that you do not miss the markets in between. If you went straight to national coverage with the media or massive exposure online overnight, you would miss the markets in between. I owned and operated a public relation firm years ago. Many clients asked me to get them on *Oprah*. My instant reply always shocked them. It was simple, "No way." To a stunned look on their face or a dead silence on the phone, I would explain. Why would you want to go directly to *Oprah* and miss the markets in between? If you look at most of the guests on *Oprah* that were instant successes, they sold millions of books, became well-known overnight, and were forgotten overnight, too. Why? Because they missed the ripple that would take them into all of the markets and in front of the additional viewers and readers in between. Rippling is vital to top-of-mind, lasting branding.

Nowadays rippling is a lot easier online because of all of the sites and outlets available for exposure. However, you need to come up with creative and forward-worthy content first so you can create some social waves. What exactly is a wave online? Think of a wave as information. The more appealing it is, the more creative and personality driven, the more likely that wave will make its way across the internet, picking up interested surfers.

A powerful wave-making approach creates what I call Top Tips— valuable advice and suggestions from you that will save someone time or money or make their lives or business easier or better. In Chapter 9, I share a template specifically designed to help you create these tips. For now, I suggest you go to content sites such as Digg.com, Squidoo.com, or Delicious.com to check out which topics got the most thumbs up on Digg, lens views on Squidoo, or made front page on Delicious.

Create compelling offers

Getting the attention of connections and prospects online is a lot easier than you might think. All you have to do is be you. I know, there should be more to it, but really there isn't. Whether you are working for a company or have your own business, you need to remember that any offers you put online to attract more attention have to come from the brand's core personality. For example, my brand is me. I have a certain lingo I use and writing style that comes from me. I am not trying to be someone else. I am just me. This is the way I talk, present, create my products, and post out offers online. Recently, I sent an email to my database with the following offer. Let's break down my approach.

There are hundreds of content creation sites available online if you do not do not have the time or do not want to create your own content. Make sure your flavor and personality are in every piece you publish, even if you do not write it. You can always ask a content writer to provide a quick write-up or sample on your topic to see if his writing style fits you and your industry or area of interest. Purecontent.com provides a free sample.

Email subject line: I would like to meet you in person!

Hello Randy,

With all the training and events I have this year in the US of A, I figure it would be a great opportunity to take you to dinner or coffee at one of my upcoming events. So, if you would like to have a one-on-one chat, here are the details as to how you can make it happen:

1. I will pick ONE winner at each event location that my team and I will take out for either dinner or some other meal to talk about your business (and YES, I will pay for it—go ahead and order lobster!). The meeting will either be a dinner, breakfast, lunch, or coffee depending on my travel flight as well as event schedule.

2. All of the events listed below are free to attend, so no purchase is necessary to enter. However, you must be present day of to win.

3. You must register on the applicable site for the event below and actually show up at the event as I will be pulling from cards submitted on the day of event.

Event Locations

Phoenix: March 24th—Register Here!

Houston: April 21st—Register Here!

Chicago: May 11th—Register Here!

Atlanta: June 15th—Register Here!

New York: July 14th—Register Here!

Los Angeles: August 16th—Register Here!

Miami: September 13th—Register Here!

P.S. Once you register, let me know by either emailing me back or sending a Tweet/ Facebook post, I wanna know who it might be. :)

I cannot WAIT to hang out with you and help your biz!

Hungry for more successes,

Starr Hall
International Speaker/Author/Marketing Advisor
Columnist for *Entrepreneur* magazine online
www.StarrHall.com
STARR HALL
.com

First, I needed to figure out what I wanted for an outcome from or response to this offer. For this offer, I wanted to entice more people to sign up for my live onsite events. Therefore I offered a one-on-one dinner or lunch. Second, I wanted to build deeper relationships with connections online and get some social activity. Social postings about this offer would not only help my news feed rankings on social sites, it would also encourage people to post on my blog in response to this offer as well as help with search engine optimization. The outcome of this email to my database list and post to my blog and social sites resulted in several thousand registrations as well as hundreds of posts, emails, and shouts-out online. While creating your offer, first ask yourself, "What do I want the outcome to be from this offer, and how can I use it to build deeper relationships and get social traction online?"

Question-posting back to your site

Another great way to make social waves online is to post out a survey or question that gets people from one site or page to interact on another. For example, if you want to increase your fans on Facebook, you can post out a question with a link back to your fan page like this: What do you like about social media? Please post your answer here (insert link, or URL, to your fan page). See Figure 2.1. The great thing about this approach is that people will have to "like" your fan page in order to post a reply and that will get you more fan connections. It also gets them to interact with you so you can get to know them through their answers (Figure 2.2). This is an excellent social wave technique that has been very powerful for me as well as clients and peers online. Try it. Then post your experience or outcome at www.facebook.com/starrhalldotcom. (See, I just did it.)

You can also do this by asking people to go back to your blog, post out a Tweet, or do what is called "DM," aka direct message, to you on Twitter. In order for them to send you a DM, you have to be following

figure 2.1–At tagging someone and posting question with link back to fan page

figure 2.2–It will post to their wall

each other, another excellent way to take the relationship to a deeper level. Text messaging outreach also works very well when you ask people questions. You can send out a text message asking your connections what they think about a topic and then either ask them to text back, or if you want online coverage, ask them to tweet you their answer. Offer them an incentive for taking the time to do so. Now when I suggest incentive, I don't mean a discount on a product. I suggest offering them something for free—a download, free tips, something that will help take

Post out offers or questions using a Twitter hashtag (for example: #dinnerwithstarr), that entices fellow Tweeters to find more information or register at your website, where the offer information is. You can also post this as a question, for example, *would you like to have #dinnerwithstarr?* You would follow that with your website link. A hashtag is used as an identity. It's a short set of words or a word to describe a group, event, offer, or cause. People on Twitter can then follow that hashtag to stay informed on the conversation about it.

the relationship to another trust level. However, with that said, if you have already built the relationship to a higher trust level, then by all means offer them a special deal on your product or service.

Power boost your information social wave

All information online or off comes in waves. I call these social waves. Some are small and barely circulate; others are mega big and can pound you almost uncontrollably. There is a method, a science, an approach to having a better chance to make these waves become larger. You can add power to your social wave by taking your content posts and creating a webpage called a "lens" on Squidoo, which includes any and all resources related to your top tips, favorite things, or topics of interest. Squidoo houses millions of pages of content, advice, and recommendations from people around the globe. These pages, or lenses, are getting high placement in search engines as well. We will learn about search engine optimization shortly, but for now just know that high placement on a search engine is a good thing. When you make your lenses, make sure you add as many keywords (tags) as you can that are related to your topic to bring in more traffic. Treat it like a blog and update it daily. This helps drive traffic to your site as well as your Squidoo lenses. You can also earn royalties from the traffic and clicks to your Squidoo lenses using Google Adwords, as well as add affiliate links related to your topic from Ebay, Amazon, CafePress, and Netflix.

Start a group or fan page

Utilizing a fan page or group on Facebook, or a group on LinkedIn, is an excellent way to position yourself or business as an expert in your field and to gather, connect, and engage on a topic of interest, whether it be in a private-member-only group or a public fan page. If you do not yet have one of these set up for your business, it is time. Yep, it is time

For updates on Facebook fan pages and groups, Twitter lists, and LinkedIn groups, visit the website update center for this book at www. socialwavebook.com.

to learn all about them, choose the best option(s) for your brand, and make it happen. Let's quickly review them.

Facebook fan page

Fan pages allow unlimited numbers of fans to join, whereas with personal profiles there is currently a 5,000 person cap. You can now switch to your fan page at anytime, so you can just post as your brand, instead of from your personal profile. You can also add administrators to help post and manage your fan page activity. Facebook offers analytics for your fan page called "Insights" that enable you to check the activity and demographics of those that join in as a fan or like your page (see Figure 2.3). Access to a page can only be restricted by certain ages and locations. If you want to remove a fan and block them individually, you will have to click on their name under the people that like you link, then click on Ban Permanently (see Figure 2.4). To create a fan page, go to facebook.com/pages/create.php.

figure 2.3–People who like, click on the "x"

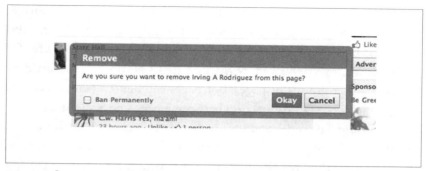

figure 2.4–Ban permanently

Facebook group

With groups you can set join permissions so they are either open to anyone, closed (where users must get administrator approval to join), or secret (invite only). Public groups can be found via Facebook search; however secret groups cannot. Groups can have administrators that manage the group, approve applicants, or invite others to join. There are now live chat features as well. To create a group you go to facebook. com/groups/create.php.

Facebook pages vs. groups: how to choose

Pages can be created to represent only real organizations, businesses, celebrities, or bands, and may be created only by an official representative of that entity. Groups can be created by anyone on about any topic as a space for people to share their opinions and interest in that subject. Groups can be kept closed or secret, whereas pages are intended to help an entity communicate publicly. Groups are generally meant for smaller numbers of people, those you know personally, and have limiting functions in place when the group members exceed a certain number. Pages are intended to be a place for organizations, businesses, celebrities, or bands to connect with users who like them. Pages can host applications, so a page can essentially be more personalized and show more content. Groups can't do this. Another key difference is that pages are indexed by external search engines such as Google and Bing, just like a public profile, while groups are not. Groups offer far more control over who gets to participate. Ads can be purchased to promote either groups or pages, but pages can benefit from social ads that publicize the fan connection between a page and a specific user.

In closing, fan pages and groups are great platforms for your loyal followers and customers to come together for your product or service, all supporting the growth of your online community. Creating a fan page or public group also gives you more footing in search-engine ranking. By publishing backlinks to your business's pages as well as having a Facebook fan page or public group with your name in the title, your business can get some bonus points when it comes to search engine optimization (SEO). Did I mention it's completely free and you can be up and running in just a few minutes?

LinkedIn groups

LinkedIn provides a wide range of tools that allow you to stay connected with your members in ways that feel personal. The "templates" feature allows you to provide automatic responses to new members and even to those requesting to join your group. It's an easy way to make new members in your community feel welcome. One of the biggest complaints about LinkedIn groups is the number of people who join simply to promote themselves or their business and then hijack the group discussion boards. They usually aren't interested in engaging with others and can have a negative impact on your community. One way to manage this type of posters is by designating a place, like a subgroup, for group members to promote their service offerings.

Subgroups are automatically available to all of your group members and are easy to set up. Highlighting this promotional opportunity satisfies those who want to self-promote and keeps your discussion boards open for business. You can also feature members in other ways,

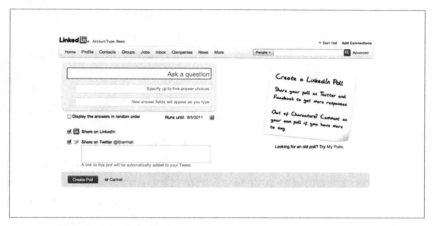

figure 2.5–LinkedIn's poll application

such as in your occasional emails to the group membership or in a featured discussion that you update regularly.

You can always add newsfeeds and post articles of interest on your topic for other members to read. You can also use LinkedIn's polls application to get feedback from your members on group features and functionality. Create a free poll and then highlight it in your group, either by linking to it on the discussion boards or by submitting the poll's URL to your News section (Figure 2.5). The member size of LinkedIn means that your group is more than likely to get some members without much effort on your part. However, I encourage you to use the promotion tools.

Fan page and group rules in general

Encourage member participation by praising and highlighting valuable contributions to your fan page or group. This motivates others to share their content and engage. If you encounter negative or counterproductive behavior from a member or fan, it's important to be professional and civil. We will look at exactly how to respond or handle this type of situation in Chapter 6, "How to Deal with the Sharks

Online." For now, know that should it become necessary to issue a warning, handle the matter privately. Apart from unusual behavior or spam, it's also a good idea to give a member a warning or two before banning her from the group.

Interactive campaigns and contests

An interactive campaign is basically the same thing as a contest or sweepstake. As long as the consumer actively has to click, answer, post, Tweet, sign up, or sing in exchange for conversation or in this instance a prize, it is considered interactive. At a time when consumers increasingly resent being marketed to, interactive promotions like sweepstakes, contests, and give-aways are a form of marketing that consumers actually like. According to Jupiter Research, an internet-based market research company, 50 percent of internet users enter sweepstakes at least once a month and 23 million Americans report that they enter contests or sweepstakes at least once a week. Interactive promotions are quickly becoming a great way to fulfill a number of marketing goals such as building a company's social network page fan base. Companies that run contests on their social network pages have twice as many fans or e-newsletter subscribers as those that don't, according to Wildfireapp.com.

There are dozens of interactive and sweepstakes campaign applications online. A couple that stand out for ease of use, results, and low to no cost, are wildfireapp.com and zoomzio.com. Make sure that the site you choose is in line with incorporating contest rules and disclosures for entries.

Businesses are recognizing the power of interactive promotions to engage social network users. Yet the majority of such promotions are advertised on the social networks but are not integrated with them. Companies need to take advantage of the social networks' viral features like friend invites, activity streams, and notifications to get the best results from interactive promotions. Such viral features have the potential to spread the word about a promotion to tens or even hundreds or more users for every one person that enters. A few different options for running an interactive campaign, whether on Facebook or another social site are:

1. *Sweepstakes.* You can launch a sweepstakes-focused campaign to give away prizes by drawings of chance. It starts with an entry form that you can design with custom pictures and graphics. Next you need to determine eligibility criteria, how long you want to run the campaign, and the prize. The main benefit on your end should be easily downloaded data gathered from participants. Sweepstakes promote responses among customers by enticing them to submit free entries for drawings. Large grand prizes tend to attract more entries, regardless of the odds of winning.

2. *Coupons.* They are a great way to engage your target market get it to consider purchasing your product or service. You can start by giving away coupons on your Facebook fan page. Coupons are a great way to make important connections with potential customers, introduce new products, and increase brand awareness and loyalty. There are several sites that allow you to publish coupons you design, input unique discount codes compatible with your website, create entry forms, send notifications to participants, and download entry data. Don't try to recreate the wheel here by coming up with your own systems; these sites have already automated this for you.

3. *Trivia tests and quizzes.* Trivia tests and quizzes offer multiple-choice questions that can help you create a word-of-mouth wave and reach a large and growing number of active users online. You can make these fun by surveying people's favorite foods, cars, hobbies, silly sayings, etc. As long as the survey is tied into your industry, have fun with it. For example, if you are a dessert food company, you can survey people or have a quiz asking people what their favorite desserts are. This is fun for your users while you gain popularity and build awareness of your company.

A few viral quizzes have been simple questions left unanswered: *What did the chicken see when she crossed the road?* or *Which is better: milk, orange juice, or apple juice?* Again, just relate the questions to something that would actually benefit your brand by having the answers. You can add fun to any trivia contest or quiz.

Focus on word of mouth

Word of mouth, or WOM, is a very powerful way to make tidal waves online. So how in heck do you get people to start talking about you or your brand in a positive light and on a viral level? How does viral happen? You are so inquisitive. I love that you asked. Let's look at a few studies behind the power of word of mouth first; then we can focus on the how.

A research report on the "Effects of Word-of-Mouth Versus Traditional Marketing," released by the American Marketing Association, showed elasticity of word-of-mouth referrals is about 20 times higher and WOM is even more sustainable than media appearances. The study also pointed out that it "may be among the most effective of marketing communication strategies." This explains why there was an increase in spending on word-of-mouth marketing by 14.2 percent ($1.54 billion) in 2009!

Another 2010 word-of-mouth study "A New Way to Measure Word-of-Mouth Marketing," released by McKinsey, which specializes in global growth management, said word of mouth is the primary factor influencing 20 to 50 percent of all purchases. McKinsey's report also noted that word of mouth can prompt a consumer to consider a brand, product, or company in a way that incremental advertising simply cannot.

A critical driver of influence is the credibility and trustworthiness of the messenger. Authentic reviews from trusted sources have a 400 percent greater impact on a recipients' purchase decision compared to low-trust sources. In order to gain the full value of creating an authentic online word-of-mouth reputation, you need to jump in and use rating sites that authenticate individual reviews. Reviews sites that have limited or no authentication process will not have the same influence because they are easy to game by lesser competitors. We will discuss review sites in just a bit, but we have a few more things to cover before we get there.

So, are you convinced about the power of WOM? If not, then take some time to search for more case studies online. For now let's figure out how you are going to make this happen for your business. First of all, WOM happens when you can get the happy voices of your customers to amplify and be your best evangelists. By sharing their success stories of using your product or service, you empower them to sway the purchase decisions of many others. Creating customer case studies prompts our human instinct to share, tell a story, and give advice. A great way to start this type of approach is to include and involve people in your message.

Next, you need to also reach out to key connectors and influencers online with which you have worked or would like to. Influential, connected customers are WOM gold mines. No matter who you reach out to, or how you involve people in your message, you need always to be upfront and transparent. Do not try to sway, bribe, or move someone to take action when it comes to word of mouth. Don't get me wrong, you can certainly ask here and there, but there is no need to con someone into talking about you. People will promote you without being asked.

I came across a post the other day from one of my online connections who had asked my opinion on a Twitter campaign. (Ugh, there is that word again—campaign. I had to use it the way that he posted it out.) Called "Why the Bing Tweet Was So Bad," it was positioned to be a cause marketing approach. However, a lot of people were highly offended by Bing's campaign. A Tweet from the @Bing Twitter account promised to donate a dollar to the Japan Earthquake Fund for every ReTweet, up to $100,000. Enlisting the help of Bing promoters and celebrities Ryan Seacrest and Alyssa Milano, the Tweet was ReTweeted many times. It was also seen, however, as a tactless attempt to cash in on the misfortunes of others, and was quickly denounced by both Tweets and blog posts, and a counter campaign was launched on Twitter using an unprintable hashtag (meaning there was use of a pretty ugly word in it), which was used well over 100 times. It was probably seen by thousands of Twitter users. The hashtaggers were outraged that Bing couldn't make a donation without asking for exposure for its Twitter account and its brand in return.

This is an example of an approach to steer clear of when it comes to word-of-mouth marketing. Do not try to grow your brand from the misfortune of others. It is bad business and just an all around yucky way to market. I don't have an issue with cause marketing, that is, a brand joining efforts with a non-profit or for-cause organization to get the word out and raise awareness and money about the cause. I think cause marketing is wonderful as long as it benefits mostly the cause

WIPEOUT

I have been getting people back to my site; however, I can't seem to keep them there or get them interested in what I have to offer.

WAVE TIP

First, you need to look at your call to actions on the pages you are sending them to, whether it is your homepage or an internal page, and check two things.

1. How many things are you asking them to do? (This should be no more than three.)
2. If they could only take one action on your site, if you could only get them to do one thing—what would it be? Remember that confusion equals no! Keep it simple; do not give the visitor too much to think about.

and the business is doing it as more of a selfless act. An example of a great cause marketing campaign was when several influential Tweeters joined in to support the Susan G. Komen Foundation Tweetathon and for eight hours did nothing but Tweet for the cause, pushing people to the donation button on the Susan G. Komen site. These Tweeters were more like cause ambassadors. They did not offer their product for less, or to donate half of the proceeds, etc. They simply used their influence to raise awareness and money for a great cause.

3

BE THE BIG FISH

step-by-step strategies on how to make
your brand stand out among the competition

> *Opportunities multiply as they are seized.*
> —Sun Tzu

Brand personality has been covered in dozens of marketing and social networking books. However, there seems to be a common area that is missed when determining what your brand personality is or should be. Your focus market will have a difficult time connecting with you if you are all over the place with your online personality.

Determine your brand personality

Split personalities online just don't seem to work, so before you start posting online and engaging with your target market, take a few moments and complete the Brand Personality Questionnaire in Figure 3.1. Is your brand an individual personality, corporate standalone, corporate personality, or product stand alone? Some examples are:

1. Would you describe the brand personality as: (check all that apply)
   - ❏ Professional, yet warm and friendly
   - ❏ Sarcastic, yet clean
   - ❏ Over the top
   - ❏ Shy and introverted
   - ❏ Outgoing and fun
   - ❏ All over the place
   - ❏ Depends on the day
   - ❏ Nice and people pleasing
   - ❏ Sharp and quick witted

2. When your brand talks to or with people, does it
   - ❏ use first person
   - ❏ use narrative
   - ❏ use different team members to talk for and represent the brand

3. In the public eye, how does the brand represent itself?
   - ❏ Stays behind the curtain and is heard but not seen
   - ❏ Stands out on stage to be seen and heard
   - ❏ Conservative, yet present
   - ❏ Loud and proud—will do anything (within reason) to be seen and heard

4. Is the brand:
   - ❏ An individual personality
   - ❏ A corporate standalone
   - ❏ A corporate personality
   - ❏ A product standalone

figure 3.1–Brand personality questionnaire

- *Oprah (Individual personality)*. Oprah represents her own brand. No one else stands in the public eye to build and/or represent the *Oprah* brand. She posts as herself, makes appearances, and writes on behalf of her brand.
- *AT&T (Corporate standalone)*. There is not one set personality representing this brand. For the most part, we do not know who the CEO is for AT&T, let alone any personality behind the brand. It does not post online as an individual, only as a brand.
- *Zappos (Corporate personality)*. CEO Tony Heish is the face of this very large and well-known brand, but he has also included his entire team to engage and represent the brand online. This brand is represented by a main personality supported by team members and supporters.
- *Whirlpool (Product standalone)*. There is no one individual or team that represents this type of brand; the product has a personality of its own. The best way to post online as a product standalone is to provide product demonstrations, facts and statistics, and an inside look at how the product is made, shipped, or was invented.

Put your answers to the personality questionnaire in one sentence. This is the personality you should be portraying online. Even if your brand is conservative, you can still have that come through with fun posts. If you are not yet clear about what your brand's online personality should be, ask some supportive friends, family, and/or clients/customers. Make sure that you do not try to be someone that you aren't. Just be you, whether serious, analytical, funny, quick-witted, curious, or playful. People online can see fake from miles away. They sense it by the way you post, the things you share (or don't share), and how you represent your brand. Nowadays, they will call you out on it, too.

Take risks to stand out

Standing out from your competition has everything to do with how willing you are to take risks, get out of your comfort zone, stand up, and be heard and seen. There is an excellent story that brings to light the benefits of taking a risk. It is a true story about a blind man trying to cross a road. He had been waiting a while at a busy road for someone to offer to guide him across when he felt a tap on his shoulder. "Excuse me," said the tapper, "I'm blind. Would you mind guiding me across the road?" The first blind man took the arm of the second blind man, and they both crossed the road. The first blind man was the jazz pianist George Shearing. He is quoted (in *Bartlett's Anecdotes*) as saying after the event, "What could I do? I took him across and it was the biggest thrill of my life."

The moral to this story is that there are times when we think we cannot do something, so we do not stretch or take a risk. Being forced to stretch and take a risk can often help us reduce our dependencies on others as well as our own personal safety mechanisms, and discover new excitement and capabilities. What risks can you take to set your brand apart from your competition? Monitor your competition to find gaps and opportunities where you could be taking risks and reaching into areas they are not covering.

Dominos' recent advertising outreach required the company to step out of its comfort zone and admit that it was wrong, it had screwed up, and it made crappy pizza. It found that people in general did not like its pizza, or Dominos was not their first choice. People only ordered its pizza because of convenience or cost, not because of quality or taste. It aimed to change that through an online and television campaign admitting that they needed to change. This transparency and approach seemed to hit home because its sales increased 14 percent according to *Ad Age*. The risk here was stepping up out of its comfort zone and being transparent by admitting that Dominos pizza was terrible. It took this message online, and the response was mostly positive. It was a scary step to take, I am sure because it is never easy to admit when you are wrong. It doesn't feel great, that is, until you come out with it, stand up, be proud, and make it happen. You take a risk walking out your door every morning, so why not take a risk to grow your brand and expand your exposure? Even if it backfires, admit it. At least you tried and you know. Then move on.

Set up competition monitors

With all of the conversations online, how in the world do you monitor what your competition is doing and saying, let alone what your focus market is saying about them or to them online? One of the best ways is to set up monitors through a social media dashboard such as Hootsuite.com. You can set up what are called "streams," or "columns," using keywords. A great approach with competition monitoring is to take care of its unhappy customers for them. Use keywords that these upset customers might use about the competition, for example, "not happy with xyz product" or "bad customer service xyz product." I set these monitors up for a mobile client of mine and within days hundreds of upset customer opportunities came across them. For a quick video on how to set these monitors up, visit the blog for this book: www. socialwavebook.com.

Another way to stay informed is to set up ego searches. Ego searches are keywords or keyword phrase searches for a specific brand, product, or company name. They are a great way to monitor mentions of a competing product. You can automate the setup of ego searches using RSS so anytime a competitor's product or brand name is mentioned in the news, blogosphere, or print, you receive notification and the details in an RSS feed. If you want to set up an RSS feed, two excellent sites have done most of the work for you: www.feedforall.com/ego-searches. htm and www.rss-tools.com/ego-search-feeds.htm.

If you need to find out exactly who your competition is, go to www.spyfu.com and enter a keyword, company name, or domain. Click the results to view the companies' top 25 competitors. If any of those websites are using pay per click on Google, you will also be able to obtain a partial list of the ad words they have purchased.

There are also a number of ways to determine who is linking to a competitor. A simple search on Yahoo! Explorer will produce all of the web pages that provide a link to your competitor. You can also check out your own site to see who is linking back to you as well. Now, if you are really web savvy or if you want to be, you can monitor your competitors' websites to find out when they make any changes. You can do this using a tool like CodeMonitor. CodeMonitor takes a snapshot of a websites' HTML and notifies you of any changes. The differences in the web pages are highlighted, making it easy to discern what changes occurred. CodeMonitor is a free online tool that can be found at https://polepositionweb.com/roi/codemonitor/index.php.

MarketLeap (www.marketleap.com/publinkpop/) is a great site to monitor the search engine activity of your competitors. It will verify search engine placement based on keywords so you can quickly determine a competitor's ranking for various phrases in the top search engines. You can also take a sneak peak at its meta tags, that is, text inserted into the source code of a web page that includes keywords that provide information to a search engine about the contents of the page for search engine optimization, by entering its url and checking it out at www.submitexpress.com/analyzer/. Pay particular attention to the header tags that include title, description, and keywords. Are these keywords part of your marketing mix?

Put your customers to work

Yes, it is OK to put your customers and/or clients to work. Often customer- or client-generated content is better than brand-generated content. By taking something as simple as frequently asked questions and turning them into valuable posts, you will not only appease your customers but also answer its questions. In order to encourage customer participation, hold contests to promote the sharing of stories, photos, and videos, and don't be cheap with the prizes. Take photos at events or tradeshows and post them online. Ask your clients or even new connections to find their photo and tag themselves, an excellent way to get them to "like" your Facebook fan page. Your customers will support you if you ask in a nonintrusive way and get them involved with your branding. They want to feel heard and appreciated. In my experience, people genuinely want to help you, especially if you start the sentence by asking, "I was wondering if you would be willing to help me," or " I am hoping that you can help." You can also make their contributions a monthly blog post topic so customers come to expect it and engage in the outreach.

For my latest business adventure, I am opening a champagne bar in Avila Beach, California (Cuvée Champagne and Delights Bar), and I plan on having iPads or tablets onsite with wifi access. We will encourage customers to Yelp or TripAdvisor about their experience, the food, etc., while they are onsite. If we ask them to do it when they get home, chances are very slim that they will remember, let alone keep the excitement and motivation to complete a review. In addition, if they do complete it onsite, we will offer a free champagne or dessert tasting, something along those yummy lines. They get a delicious treat and we get a scrumptious review. And this is a win-win for both the customer and the brand. If you are going to do something like this onsite, do not depend on the customer's mobile phone connection. Provide it for them so there are no access or connection issues. Make it as simple as possible for them to write a review about their experience. The more complicated you make it, the less likely they are to actually do it.

I have found that people genuinely like to give me testimonials on video camera whenever I have an event. Yes, it could be due to the fact that we have the camera right in their face and put them on the spot, but, hey, they say it with a smile and their testimonial is golden. Take those videos and post them on your blog. Make sure that you ask the person while recording if you have permission to post on your blog and on the internet; if they say no, then ask them if you can translate the video script into copy and post. You can also create a testimonials section somewhere on that site of yours, and *voilà*, fresh content. You

can see several of mine under the "Book Starr Hall" section at www.
starrhall.com.

Send personal replies

When you first send an invite to connect with someone, whether you
know them or not, add a personal note into the request. If you do know
them, bring up a good or funny memory from the past. If you do not yet
know them, quickly browse the information in their profile, and pick
out something you can genuinely comment about—a common interest
or a post that got your attention. It might even be mention of a mutual
connection. If you take the time to add an extra, personal touch, you
have a better chance of staying top of mind with them when they read
your posts in the newsfeed.

The same applies when you accept a request as well. Wouldn't
it be nice, instead of getting the standard email from LinkedIn that
says your connection request has been accepted, you received a quick
note that says, "Thank you for the connection. I see you live in LA. I
was born and raised there. Look forward to reading your posts." You
don't just walk up to someone at a meeting or event and not add some
form of personable greeting, correct? So why would you do it online?
I know what you are thinking, "But Starr, that takes sooooo much
time." To that I reply, "Yes, it does take a bit more time, but you are
building relationships here, remember, not numbers." Also remember
that taking this time really helps both people get to know each other
just a little bit more. These personal notes can lead to an opportunity
or maybe even a referral. Is that worth a few extra minutes of your time
here and there? You bet.

Build and seed your network

After you are done reading this book, I don't want you to just build your
network once and then not revisit it for a year or until your sales are
declining next spring. You need to constantly be building your network.

For those of you who are new or getting ready to launch a new passion business, I suggest that you build your network before you launch your business. I read about a site recently that did just that. Before launching MyWorkButterfly, a site for working moms and moms wanting to return to the workforce, Bradi Nathan and Terry Starr conducted a National Moms Survey on Facebook. The two women pushed the survey out to everyone they knew and asked those people to push it out to everyone they knew. The goal of the survey was to find out what moms would want from a moms social network. The feedback they got from that survey became the playbook for all the content and design of MyWorkButterfly. Sections such as job listings, personalized welcome messages, and even the order of the drop-down menu items came directly from that survey. In addition, those initial survey takers became MyWorkButterfly's first users and since they could see their voice was heard, they quickly became very supportive of the site. Only three months after launching, MyWorkButterfly claimed 2,000 members and 40,000-plus page views a month with over a six-minute average time on site per visit.

There are dozens of ways that you can reach out to new connections presented in this book. There are several scripts to get you started, beginning on page 89. Make sure you make the scripts your own, again by adding in your brand personality. But no matter how you use them, get out there and connect. Commit to a personal goal to meet x number of new connections every month, a number of people who you can personally get to know and maintain a connection with the ongoing building of your network. You need to set a number you feel will work for you. Whether it is 25 per week or month, the goal has to be set. Without a goal, you will never know when you get to your marketing destination, let alone how.

Every time you have an event, give an onsite training, or provide a webcast online, make sure you have some type of reach-out system in place. Whether you ask them to sign up for the webcast so you can have their contact info or get their cards at an event by offering them access for a limited time to your VIP business-building club, there is always a way to gather their info. Some events can get you hundreds of cards in a matter of minutes. Take them back to the office, use a card scanner that sends them into an Excel document, and then upload them to your email program. Guess what comes next? Your automated yet personalized email is ready to go as soon as those cards are uploaded. The process from your event to email need take no more than 72 hours to turn around and reach out to the connections so you can start to build a relationship. It's smart to start building immediately, while you are at top of mind. OK, if you get stuck on an airplane, or live in an airport for 72 hours in Denver, Colorado, because of bad weather, with no luggage, the process takes a little bit longer, but you get the point.

Moving onward, once you make that initial reach out, you need to make sure you seed your network. That means you need to stay in touch with your connections. You'll see how, in Chapter 13, Anchoring Online Relationships, where we talk all about email marketing. Whoo, this is fun, isn't it! In the interim, let's talk about how you can be selective with your networking online. This will save you a ton of time when building relationships.

The broker/owner of Platinum Realty Network in Scottsdale, Arizona, Pete Baldwin, was only interested in growing his social network with real estate enthusiasts interested in country clubs, golf, or mountain retreat custom log homes. We began his campaign searching for country club users in Scottsdale, as well as golf trade associations that were on Twitter or Facebook. We mined the lists of people they were following, looking for golf pros, skiing enthusiasts, country club conversations, golf blogs, golf writers, and media outlets. This required a lot of research, clicking through and reading bios of many users. To get followed back to Pete's network, it was important that we read posts, interacted, and started dialogues. We quickly realized those who chose not to follow Pete back were not interested in interacting with him, so we would "unfollow" those people. It was a lot of hard work, but at the end of three months Pete had set up several cross-marketing projects, set up new client or agent recruitment meetings, attracted two national media writers, four local papers and magazines were interested in having him blog. Today, Pete's Twitter account @prnarizona has more than 1,500 highly targeted followers.

WIPEOUT

I have no idea what to post online. I always think that no one cares what I have to say, spend ten minutes thinking about what to post, then I do not post anything. What can I do to get me posting more online?

WAVE TIP

First of all, do not worry about whether people will care about what you have to say. You need to be you, just as if the person was in front of you. The more you share your personality, the more people connect and remember at a deeper level. People do care what you are eating, where you are at, and where you are going; that is how they connect with you psychologically. Try posting things that you are doing throughout the day with a little humor in it. Ex: "Just mowed the lawn, will now cash in on allowance for doing my son's job. Momma needs a new pair of shoes!"

4

STOP PADDLING UPSTREAM, START SAILING

how to set up social marketing systems,
including social media policies and procedures

> Action will
> destroy your
> procrastination.
> —Og Mandino

This section really should have been in
the very first paragraphs of this book. I actually went back and forth
several times about where to talk about building your foundation.
So, why did it end up all the way here in this chapter? I decided to
get you motivated before I started to talk about how to set your
foundation online.

Set your foundation

So what exactly am I referring to? I am so glad you asked. I am
specifically talking about your website. When you start to get active
and social online, what is your ultimate goal? I am hoping that
somewhere in there it is to get people back to your website so they
can learn more about you and ultimately engage with you. With this
goal in mind, you need to make sure your website foundation is set

with a solid footing and a structure. Let's take a look at a few things on your website right now.

First of all, when you go to your website using different web browsers—Safari, Internet Explorer, and Firefox—how is does your website look? Is it consistent on all browsers? Are you seeing the same thing every time? If not, you need to pull your web designer and/or master in and let them know. You need to make sure your site is as consistent as possible. Next, is there a balance between copy, visuals, and video? If you have more than one paragraph on your homepage, you just might have too much. If you have nothing but pictures, then you need to go in and add that paragraph. Really, you don't even need that paragraph, you can have just calls to action telling visitors exactly what you would like them to do, of course with a very inviting and friendly presence. We will cover calls to action in Chapter 13, but for now just look at the balance of your homepage, as well as your site, overall. If you have any evidence of clipart, or text running off of the screen, please look at other options. See Chapter 7 for sites based on WordPress, a powerful blogging platform with amazing and affordable (many are free) template design options.

Last, but not least, you need to have some way to gather visitors' contact information so you can keep in touch with them on an ongoing basis, which we will get into in depth later. For now, start looking at your website foundation. Ask yourself this very simple and basic question, "Would I navigate through this site?" If you answered yes to that, then I want you to consider surveying other people that will give you their honest opinion. This means people in your center of influence that you know will not just tell you what you want to hear. See Figure 4.1 for a sample survey. There are some excellent, free and low-cost survey-generating sites and programs that will send a few basic questions out to your connections, clients, friends, and neighbors. Survey Monkey and Zoomerang are two popular survey-generating sites.

Remember that when you are creating or remodeling a website, it's easy to think people are going to scrutinize each page thoughtfully,

I am working on improving my website so it can give visitors a better experience. I would like what we do to be clearly communicated on the homepage and throughout the site. With this in mind, would you please take a few minutes to visit my website and answer a few survey questions? I will send you a gift for taking the time to help me with your valuable feedback.

1. When you land on the homepage, what draws your attention first?

   _____

   _____

   _____

2. Just looking at the homepage, what do you think our business does?

   _____

   _____

   _____

3. Does the homepage clearly define what our company does?
   ○ Yes
   ○ No

4. Do you feel like you want to look throughout the site after looking at the homepage?
   ○ Yes
   ○ No

5. On a scale of 1–10, how simple is this site to navigate? (1 being absolutely frustrating; 10 being excellently simple)

1	2	3	4	5	6	7	8	9	10
○	○	○	○	○	○	○	○	○	○

figure 4.1–Sample website survey

6. If you were looking for this service or product, would you purchase it from or do business with this site?

○ Yes

○ No

Please explain your answer:

_____

_____

_____

7. How is the quantity of copy on the site?

○ Not enough copy

○ Too much copy

○ Just right

8. Are there enough visual graphics and pictures throughout the site?

○ Not enough imagery

○ Too much imagery

○ Just right

Any additional feedback

_____

_____

_____

_____

figure 4.1–Sample website survey, continued

reading your carefully chosen words and phrases. What people often do, in reality, is scan each page and click on the first thing that resembles what they're looking for. If it is too complicated, or if they have to think or navigate too much, then they are "outta there!" Less is more when it comes to your website foundation.

Set automated systems

The word "automated," when used in the context of marketing, often connotes that it is nonpersonal. However, setting up automated systems does not mean making your company robotic. You can set up systems that set standards for consistency as well as efficiency so you and your team of supporters are all on the same page. You all know what to do, when to do it, and how to improve it. Three key areas need to be developed when setting up automation for your online marketing.

1. *Policies and procedures.* This document and agreement includes specific direction about what everyone involved in or with your brand can and cannot do online and off when it comes to representing the brand; this includes vendors, employees, and even your family, if they are involved.
2. *Follow-through system.* This system or program should focus on determining and capturing leads, and includes contact management as well as ongoing communications via email and online.
3. *Assessment system.* An analytics system for your online efforts so you can assess what is working and what is not.

Policies and procedures

When it comes to policies and procedures for your team members, do not forget that times have changed with the information age. You now need to include vendors, as well as family members, if they are involved with your business at any level. If you are connected to one of your children on a social site, they should review and agree to your online practices, because they are an extension of your brand. The same thing applies to vendors if they want to do business with you or are connected to you online. Send them a copy to read and sign as well.

If you think this is something you can develop when you have time to get around to it, consider the example of a brand that you just might know—United Airlines. When United Airlines customer Dave Carroll's $2,500 guitar was broken while traveling via their service on his way to a gig with his band, he started to produce music videos about United Airlines that have each now been viewed by up to 11 million people. United Airlines did not have effective social media policies and procedures in place advising team members on what they were allowed to do in order to make this situation right with Dave Carroll. Furthermore, when Dave's videos started to go viral on the internet, United Airlines had no solid plan for turning their gaffe into an opportunity to reach out to their customers and demonstrate their superior customer service. To date it has been reported on numerous sites and blogs that it has cost United Airlines upwards of $20 million for this mishap. To view these videos, go to YouTube and search on "United Breaks Guitars" or visit the blog for this book at www.socialwavebook.com to view all three videos. Another example is Domino's Pizza. Two of its employees decided to post videos on the internet showing the disgusting things that they did while making pizzas.

These stories are classic examples of the need for a policies and procedures in place, as well as a damage control plan, should you have any shakeups online. We will learn about damage control in Chapter 6. For now, let's get your social media and online policies and procedures in place. A social media policies and procedures will not assure that nothing bad happens or that it will keep employees from acting out online or not representing the brand properly, but it certainly helps to have an understanding in place for all involved, a support system, as well as clearly-stated and enforceable consequences, should certain policies not be followed.

When you are putting your policies together, consider allowing employees the freedom to make things right with customers online (or off), should they have a bad experience. Zappos is an excellent example of how powerful customer service can enhance a brand, allowing its employees to refund, send additional items, and make decisions without higher up approval so the customers experience is a good one. Happy customers Tweet, they go on Yelp, a customer experience review site, and they will post anywhere and everywhere they have access, so you have to make sure that their experience is not just good, but great. It is this kind of word of mouth that can drive a brand viral. Don't worry; we will look at word-of-mouth techniques in Chapter 12.

SAMPLE SOCIAL MEDIA POLICIES AND PROCEDURES

We strongly suggest you give consideration to your own standards, industry culture, and legal practices for your firm. Please note that it is equally important to be familiar with the ethics rules of the states in which you operate. We advise you to seek legal counsel in finalizing your social media and online policies and procedures prior to releasing them to your staff, independent contractors, vendors, and consultants.

INTELLECTUAL PROPERTY NOTICE

The material contained here may be protected under various intellectual property laws, including copyright and trademark. Unless otherwise stated, this material is and remains the intellectual property of Starr Hall LLC, and all rights are reserved. No part of this material may be incorporated, reproduced, republished, distributed, transmitted, displayed, broadcast, or otherwise exploited in any manner, except for the internal use and analysis by the requesting firm, without the express prior written permission of Starr Hall LLC. The Starr Hall logos, related trademarks, and other intellectual property are the property of Starr Hall LLC and cannot be used without its express prior written permission. Copyright © 2010–2011 StarrHall.com. All rights reserved.

(INSERT YOUR COMPANY NAME) SOCIAL MEDIA
AND SOCIAL NETWORKING POLICIES AND PROCEDURES

NOTE: First make sure you include an introduction into your policies and procedures.

[Insert your company address]

As a company, we believe that social media can drive business and support your professional development efforts. We are also aware that social media use will not be exclusively for business.

Keeping that in mind, we attempt here to provide reasonable guidelines for online behavior by members (including, but not limited to, staff, independent contractors, affiliates, and directors) of our company when participating online on behalf of our brand.

figure 4.2–Sample social media policies and procedures

As new tools on the web are introduced and new challenges emerge for all of us, this document will, of necessity, evolve.

Below represents the Company's current policy regarding social media and social networking.

Your Identity Online

You are responsible for what you post. You are personally responsible for any of your online activity conducted with a Company email address and/or which can be traced back to the company's domain, brand name, and/or which uses company assets. The (company's domain name).com address attached to your name implies that you are acting on the company's behalf. When using Company email, or Company assets to engage in any social media or professional social networking activity (for example, LinkedIn and Plaxo), all actions are public, and staff and associates will be held fully responsible for any and all said activities. All emails using the Company's name or identity are public internally and property of the Company ongoing.

Outside the workplace, your rights to privacy and free speech protect online activity conducted on your personal social networks with your personal email address. However, what you publish on such personal online sites should never be attributed to the company and should not appear to be endorsed by or originated from the Company. If you choose to list your work affiliation on a social network, then you should regard all communication on that network as you would in a professional network. Online lives are ultimately linked, whether or not you choose to mention the company in your personal online networking activity.

Be transparent. When participating in any online community, disclose your identity and affiliation with the Company and your professional and/or personal interest. When posting to a blog, always use your name. Never create an alias, and never be anonymous.

Follow the rules in the Company's employee manual. These rules also apply to employee behavior within social networking and other public online spaces.

figure 4.2–Sample social media policies and procedures, continued

Follow the terms and conditions of use that have been established by each venue used for your social networking activities.

Obey the law. Don't post any information or conduct any online activity that may violate applicable local, state, or federal laws or regulations.

Never be false and misleading in your online credentials. Staff members [insert "consultants" or "distributors," as applicable] must maintain complete accuracy in all of their online biographies and ensure there is no embellishment.

Creating and Managing Content

Be direct, informative, and brief. Never use a Company customer's or client's name in a blog posting, unless you have written permission to do so.

Credit appropriately. Identify all copyrighted or borrowed material with citations and links. When publishing any material online that includes another's direct or paraphrased quotes, thoughts, ideas, photos, or videos, always give credit to the original material or author, where applicable.

Fact-check your posts. Always evaluate your contribution's accuracy and truthfulness. Before posting any online material, ensure that the material is accurate, truthful, and without factual error.

Spell and grammar check everything. Content never disappears entirely once it's been posted.

Correct errors promptly. If you find that your blog entry contains an error or mistake, correct it. Since transparency is key, admit your mistake, apologize if necessary, correct it, and move on.

While a blog itself is not subject to the limitation on commercial speech, the content of a blog can be. The content must be informative only, and nothing in the content should propose a commercial transaction or be for the purpose of directly gaining a commercial transaction.

(Your company may want to insert screen shots of approved posts or content in this section.)

figure 4.2–Sample social media policies and procedures, continued

Leaving Comments

When posting to a blog, we suggest that you refrain from posting about controversial or potentially inflammatory subjects, including politics, sex, religion, or any other nonbusiness related subjects. However, if you do express either a political or religious opinion, or an opinion regarding the Company's actions, you must include a disclaimer. Your disclaimer should specifically state that the opinion is his/her personal opinion, and not the Company's position. This is necessary to preserve the Company's goodwill in the marketplace.

In addition, the associate and/or employee, as well as the Company can be fined for any post about the Company or its products that is considered misleading. Consequently, an associate should be sure that any post to a site about the Company or its products a) is truthful, b) supported by facts, and c) discloses that the associate is employed by the company.

Any conduct which is impermissible under the law if expressed in any other form or forum is impermissible if expressed through a post on a Site. For example, posted material that is discriminatory, harassing, obscene, defamatory, libelous, or threatening is forbidden. Company policies apply equally to associate and/or employee blogging. Associates and/or employees should review the Company handbook for further guidance.

Keep the tone of your comments respectful and informative, never condescending or "loud." Use sentence case format, not capital letters. Stick to this maxim whenever you are contributing to any blogs or social and professional networks.

Avoid personal attacks, online fights, and hostile communications. If a blogger or any other online influencer posts a statement with which you disagree, voice your opinion, but do not escalate the conversation to a heated argument. Write reasonably, factually, and with good humor. Understand and credit the other person's point of view, and avoid any communications that could result in personal, professional, or credibility attacks. Never disclose information that is proprietary or confidential to the Company.

figure 4.2–Sample social media policies and procedures, continued

When appropriate and possible, provide a link to your LinkedIn or Xing Profile (or other professional networks online), or to supporting documents. This will help raise your Google results as well as the brand. If in doubt, don't!

Confidentiality and Privacy

Don't disclose confidential information. Honor the terms of your contracts with the Company and contracts we have with any clients, vendors, or customers. Do not disclose or use confidential or proprietary information of the Company or any client, vendor, or customer in any form of online media. Sharing this type of information, even unintentionally, can result in legal action against you, the Company, and/or the client. Any information that cannot be disclosed through a conversation, a note, or an email also cannot be disclosed on a site.

Avoid forums where there is little control over what you know to be confidential information. In the world of social networking, there is often a breach of confidentiality when someone emails a legal or financial contact or posts a comment congratulating him/her on representation of a specific client or on a specific case or client portfolio. Often these things are being discussed in the social network circles, so be very selective and thoughtful about where you post and how you reply (or not).

Respect the opinions of others and the privacy of your co-workers, employees, and peers, as well as associates. Before sharing a comment, post, picture, or video about a co-worker, employee, peer, or associate through any type of social media or network, his/her consent is not only a courtesy, it is a requirement.

Potential Conflicts and Red Flags

Get approval for a post when:

- *Responding to a negative post.* If a blogger or any other online participant posts an inaccurate, accusatory, or negative comment about the Company, or any client, vendor, consultant, or associate, do not engage in the conversation without prior approval of (name of person authorized to give this approval).

figure 4.2–Sample social media policies and procedures, continued

4 / stop paddling upstream, start sailing

- *Posting recommendations for colleagues.* Posting recommendations of colleagues is a tool of professional social networking sites. The recommendations and comments you post about other current and former companies can have consequences, even if you are associated with the Company in the past x number of years.
- *If you are contacted directly by a journalist.* Regarding issues of concern to the Company, clear the query with [name of person authorized to give this approval] before responding to any journalist.

Other Potential Red Flag Situations

Use a disclaimer if you communicate electronically about fees, awards, recent cases, or case outcomes. (NOTE TO COMPANY: Do you want to require prior approval for this?)

We ask that you clear all potential recommendations and comments with [name of person authorized to give this approval], for anyone who is or was ever associated with the company. (NOTE: Use of a company approved disclaimer may be appropriate.)

Building Your Virtual Footprint and Network

Build a reputation of trust among your contacts online in the media as well as the general public. When you are reaching out to journalists, bloggers, clients, or colleagues through social media, take every opportunity to build a reputation of trust and establish yourself as a credible and transparent professional. Don't use your own personal online relationships or the Company's network to influence polls, rankings, or web traffic.

When using social networks with your Company email and professional identification, do not "friend" anyone who you either do not actually know and/or with whom you have not previously corresponded.

Leaving the Company (Exit Policy)

Upon leaving the Company, use of the name, brand/or current employees, associates, vendors, or directors is prohibited unless you are using name in good faith and in past employer or employment history sections on social sites and public resumes. If at any

figure 4.2–Sample social media policies and procedures, continued time after your departure from the company you post derogatory remarks or anything that could be considered potentially damaging to the company's reputation and good standing, you must immediately remove company name from all public viewing within your profiles and posts.

Mediation

In the event that the parties cannot, by exercise of their best efforts, resolve any disputes in regard to social media posting, policies, and procedures, they shall submit the dispute to mediation. The parties shall, without delay, continue to perform their respective obligations under this agreement which are not affected by the dispute. The invoking party shall give to the other party written notice of its decision to do so, including a description of the issues subject to the dispute, and a proposed resolution thereof. Designated representatives of both parties shall attempt to resolve the dispute within thirty (30) days after such notice. If the dispute is not resolved 30 days, the dispute shall be submitted to binding arbitration in accordance with the arbitration provision of this agreement.

ARBITRATION

Any controversies or disputes arising out of or relating to this agreement shall be resolved by binding arbitration in accordance with the then current Commercial Arbitration Rules of the American Arbitration Association. The parties shall endeavor to select a mutually acceptable arbitrator knowledgeable about issues relating to the subject matter of this Agreement. In the event the parties are unable to agree to such a selection, each party will select an arbitrator and the arbitrators in turn shall select a third arbitrator. The arbitration shall take place at the corporate headquarters county of operation for [insert Company name here], or another location otherwise mutually agreed upon by the parties. All initial filing fees will be split equally between the parties.

The award rendered by the arbitrator shall be final and binding on the parties, and judgment may be entered thereon in any court having jurisdiction. The agreement to

figure 4.2–Sample social media policies and procedures, continued

arbitration shall be specifically enforceable under prevailing arbitration law. During the continuance of any arbitration proceeding, the parties shall continue to perform their respective obligations under this Agreement, if any.

If either party seeks to enforce the Agreement, or resolve any other dispute arising out of the Agreement, through mediation, arbitration, judicial, or other proceeding, the prevailing party shall be entitled to recover its reasonable costs and expenses (including attorneys' fees, arbitrators' fees, and expert witness fees, costs of investigation and proof of facts, court costs, other arbitration or litigation expenses, and travel and living expenses) incurred in connection with such arbitration, judicial, or other proceeding, including the costs of enforcing this provision.

In Conclusion

The Company encourages all associates to keep in mind the speed and manner in which information posted on a Site can be relayed and often misunderstood by readers. While an associate/employee's free time is generally not subject to any restrictions by the Company—with the exception of the limited restrictions in this document—the Company urges all associates to refrain from posting information regarding the Company or their jobs that could embarrass or upset other associates/employees or that could detrimentally affect the Company's relationship with its customers, its vendors, and the public. Use your best judgment. Associates/employees with any questions should review the guidelines in this document and/or consult with a manager or representative of the Company. Failure to follow these guidelines may result in discipline, up to and including termination.

By signing my name I attest that I have read this agreement completely and understand its terms, all of my questions have been answered and I agree to abide by these policies and procedures.

_____

_____

figure 4.2–Sample social media policies and procedures, continued

Today, social media encompasses a broad sweep of online activity, all of which can be tracked and traced, which can be either positive or detrimental to a brand. These networks include not only the blogs you write and those to which you comment, but also social networks such as Facebook, Squidoo, and Twitter; professional networks such as LinkedIn and Xing; and social bookmarking such as Digg and Delicious. Every day, it seems, new online tools and new advances surface allowing companies new opportunities to build their online presence.

When dealing with Creating and Managing Content, always tell them what they can post as well, give them permission to be a voice for your brand.

Check your industry and/or association's particular prohibitions against and/or limitations on testimonials before posting them online.

Constructing your follow-through system

Follow-through does not just happen once after initial contact, it is ongoing. Let's do a quick check on your follow-through system from the first point of contact either in person or on your website. Start with your website. As visitors start to land on your homepage or the inner pages of your site, follow-through begins. First ask yourself, "What do I want them to do?" Once you come up with the answer, you then need to create a call to action, or CTA, to call them or move them into taking the next step or action on your site.

Without a call to action, you are just expecting visitors to decide where they want to go once they get there. This is a huge problem with the majority of websites out there. They expect people to know what they want when they get to their site, or they offer them so many options that the visitor gets overwhelmed and leaves. You need to guide them through, step by step, and tell them what to do. Furthermore, if you want to get their name and email so you can keep in touch with them, I suggest that you have a valuable offer or giveaway that will make them want to give you their contact information. We will talk more about what this offer should be and how to create it in just a bit. For now, you need to walk yourself through your own follow-through system. Once you have built visitors' trust by offering them a valuable report or download with top tips and not bombarding them with sales bitching on your homepage, chances are they will give you their information to keep in touch and to receive more information about your products and/or service—if they like what they read or received.

Now that you have their information, what are you going to do with it? You need to get serious and set up or subscribe to an email management system or software. There are many to choose from, so you need to decide which one is right for your follow-through plan. Here are a few things to consider when looking for an email system.

First of all, how large is your email list? If you are just starting to collect emails, or if your list is under 2,500, consider using constantcontact.com, mailchimp.com, or aweber.com. For lists over 2,500, you might want to look at Infusionsoft or Exact Target. The difference between the two levels is not merely contact list management capabilities; the higher-level email management systems also offer what is called "behavioral marketing," and both offer auto-set email capabilities so you can preprogram email releases.

With behavioral marketing, when you send an email out, you would add a few link options for your contacts to click on that will tell you more about their interests. For example, if you send a link out with tips on how your contacts can save money using your service and another link on how they can save time, you can tell what they are more interested in by the option they click on. If they click on the saving money link, you would then send them into an email marketing series based on that interest.

With both levels of email service maintenance, you can auto-set emails to go out at later times. This efficiency enables you to spend one day at the beginning of every year creating your foundational email releases so you do not have to worry about creating them throughout the year. Do read them before they go out to make sure that the information is still correct or to add something new into them, and be confident that the foundation is set. The emails are ready to go out—always. What type of emails are you going to send out? Text, video, or a combination of both? If you are considering the pizzazz of video, then I suggest that you check out TalkFusion (www.TalkFusion.com/1171659). Starting around $35 a month, the service allows you to send out video emails and have video conferences, live video broadcasts, and access to its wall where you can post your video email messages for others to view. One of the main benefits of TalkFusion is its personalized templates for video emails, its simplicity, and its analytics system where you can find out who is viewing your video email and who is deleted them or not viewing them at all. You can always ask your prospects and customers how they prefer to be communicated to—video or text email? Let them tell you instead of guessing.

Implement an assessment system

As you move along in your shiny speedboat building your brand presence online, now and then you need to stop and assess what is working and what is not. By setting up analytics systems, you can monitor and determine your best practices and approaches as well as those that are just not working. Google analytics at www.google.com/analytics is an excellent and free resource from Google. You can copy and paste its analytics code onto the back end of your site so you can check out how many web visitors you get daily, weekly, and monthly, and where they are coming from in regard to traffic sources such as Facebook, search engines, and referring sites. You can also find out what keywords are working and which ones are not. It also tells how long someone views a page on your site or if that person comes to your homepage and does what is called "bounce off" right away, which means that you are not keeping their attention. The higher the bounce rate, the more people are leaving your site without going deeper. However, be aware that a high bounce rate is not always the most accurate measure.

If you are actively focused on search engine optimization, then search engines spiders (maybe they freak you out, but it is "the web," after all!) will land on your homepage to index your site and then immediately bounce or leave from the homepage. That can cause your bounce rate to be inaccurate.

Another free service that Google offers is online alerts via www.google.com/alerts. You can set up alerts to be sent to you via Google any time someone mentions your company name or posts about your product or service, or that of your competitors. This is a great way to assess activity and conversations online.

Liveperson.com is a real-time analytics service that enables you to monitor your site activity in real time and capture visitors' behaviors. You can also identify hot prospects based on visitor attributes and browser behavior, as well as engage these prospects with targeted communications and offers. Liveperson does offer a free trial and demo, but this is a paid-for tool.

These analytics and assessment tools are great for your website activity, but you should also assess your postings on social sites whenever possible to see what is generating interest. You can build campaigns or future posts and messages around popular posts. Social media dashboards such as Hootsuite and Tweetdeck offer excellent tracking and analytic tools. When you are using a dashboard, any time your post includes a website URL you can "tiny it" by using their tiny tool or go to an outside sites such as bit.ly. Not only does bit.ly shrink the web URL, which is great when you have limited amount of characters that you can post, it also offers analytics telling you how many people clicked on it. Certain tiny URL sites also offer timelines as to when the most click activity happened for the link posted.

Spend at least an hour every single week checking your online analytics to find out what worked and what didn't. This is how you determine what your focus markets needs are, where their interests are currently, and how you can create more posts and/or products to fill these needs. It also allows you to make necessary changes to your site. If your bounce rate gets high or if your site visitors drop, try playing with your site messaging and visuals, as well as postings back to your site, to improve results for the next week. If you do not assess your marketing online, you might as well throw all of your efforts to the wind and just hope that something sticks. That's called "marketing by default," and not the most effective way to grow a brand.

Deciding on your marketing budget

As much as you would love for everything to be free, when it comes to growing your business, no matter which way you try to dice it and slice it, you will eventually need to invest financially in the growth of your brand. Whether it is the printing of fliers, the customization design for your social sites, or paying a virtual marketing assistant (VMA) to implement and manage your marketing for you, you need to commit to a budget. Otherwise, you are turning your business into a hobby, or keeping it at that level. Hobbies don't make a lot of moola. I mean I like to cook. However if I tried to sell my food, I might be disappointed. If I invested in top ingredients, high-level cooking lessons, how to measure and cost food properly, as well as market my dish creations, then I am cooking with some marketing fire. Martha Stewart is an excellent example as to how she turned her commitment as a housewife and love for entertaining into a household brand by being an active marketer. She continued to reach out to new people, the media, created different marketing campaigns, held parties, invited influential people and kept on taking her brand to higher levels. She allocated money to her marketing budget as well as time to her marketing schedule. Her commitment to ongoing marketing is what made her brand today and what continues to drive her into new markets. Her initial marketing budgets were small, however

An outsourcing company to check out is 123employee.com. It offers free assistant trials as well as packages for budgets large and small.

she made it work with what she had and I am sure to this day she allocates funds for her ongoing marketing.

The days of people claiming that social media is a free marketing tool are over. They never really were. When you first jump in online, you spend a heck of a lot of time growing your presence, network, and business; Your time is billable, so all that activity is an investment in the growth of your brand. As you begin to become so busy that you need to start outsourcing, set your marketing and outsourcing budget at 10 percent of your current gross revenue. Some companies commit between 20 and 40 percent annually to their marketing budget. Why? Because they know that without marketing to grow their business, they really do not have much going on, and they must keep the marketing wheel turning to get places. Guess what? You need to do it, too.

Outsourcing all this stuff

Times have changed messaging, marketing, and your life, so you really should consider changing the way you handle tasks and services for your company. Outsourcing is becoming a very effective way to handle your online marketing. I have trained hundreds of at-home marketing people that were previously marketing executives, but now want to work from the comfort of their own home office. I call them MVAs, which stands for "marketing virtual assistants." If you find the right one, they can do wonders for your time and action management calendar, as well as help bring in the revenue.

Let's go through a list of what you should do when you are seriously considering outsourcing your online marketing to a MVA.

1. *Ask for referrals.* Talk to other small business owners for whom the MVA has provided

Some sites to find MVAs are secretstaff. com, guru.com, and, of course, you can always head over to the association for their industry, www.ivaa. org, the URL for the International Virtual Assistant Association. Jump on the phone and talk to the staff, to ask them who their top 10 most active members are.

online marketing services, and ask a few key questions: How is their creativity? Are they proactive, self-starters? Do they need handholding? Do they get you results, and if so, what type of results—an increase in revenue, time savings, better organization, or brand exposure? Are they easy and fun to work with? Do they complete actions on deadline?

2. *Check to see what software they use.* Are their software and applications compatible with those you use? If not, could they be easily trained to use your software?

3. *What types of tasks do they do and what actions do they take?* Again, a willing VA can be trained, but a MVA should have a solid background in marketing so you do not have to take them through the how-to of growing your business. Administrative tasks are one thing; marketing know-how is something completely different.

4. *What are their rates?* These vary greatly in the online world. You will see MVAs from India for $4 per hour, and in the United States they start around $20 hour going up to $100 plus. Some may charge per project or use a monthly results retainer instead of an hourly fee. In most people's experience, you do get what you pay for. When outsourcing to other countries, you need to be aware of cultural differences when it comes to marketing. Cultures are very different in terms of language, time zones, cultural knowledge, and yes, even marketing messages. If you plan on working with a MVA on an ongoing basis (as you should), an hourly agreement simplifies the process. But ask if there are any discounts available if you keep them on a MVA retainer.

5. *Test them before agreeing to a retainer.* Ideally, you do want to work with a MVA on an ongoing basis, but be sure you are a good fit in regard to personality and industry knowledge before doing so. Give him/her a few projects and make sure he/she responds in a timely manner, takes direction well, clarifies any details that need clarifying, and completes projects on time.

6. *MVA vs. freelance.* When looking for a MVA, this distinction can be tricky because a marketing virtual assistant in business is different from a freelancer. Generally speaking, a virtual assistant who is solely in the business of being a virtual assistant should be able to provide dedicated services to your business. Freelancers are generally individuals who are simply looking for steady administrative work from home, sometimes from one company, sometimes from many. Freelancers often charge less, but there are greater risks involved because they may not have the professional experience required from the modern-day MVA. There can also be tax implications if you hire a freelancer and she or he is not working for other clients. In many jurisdictions, this makes the freelancer a legal employee, which could see you liable for payroll tax and other associated costs of hiring an employee, so check with your accountant.

   You also need to beware of MVAs that do VA work on the side while trying to build another business of their own or to fill in a gap between jobs. You can then run into trouble with consistency, meeting deadlines, etc. You want to find a MVA that is committed to providing support to your business, not someone who is trying to pay the bills in the meantime.

7. *Check references.* Your virtual assistant will have access to personal and business information, so it's important to check on any references provided. You should also search Google for any reviews of their service as well as their LinkedIn profile. If they do not have a powered up LinkedIn profile, you might want to run for the door—or just hang up the phone.

8. *Certification isn't necessary.* Although certified MVAs may disagree, certification is not necessarily an indicator of an exemplary service provider. In addition, the lack of certification is not necessarily an indicator of poor service. Just go with your gut instinct. A good VA will be very involved in your business and be happy to do so. Check to make sure his/her personality is suited to your

own and you can see yourself working with him/her in the long term. This is where your own instinct comes in. If it doesn't work out, there's no need to rule out the idea of working with a VA. There are plenty of amazing VAs out there.

Figure 4.3 provides a sample MVA contract. As always, check with your legal counsel before you print and issue this to your prospective MVA. Every county, state, and country has different rules when it comes to contracts. This is just a blueprint to help you get started.

SAMPLE MVA CONTRACT

MARKETING VIRTUAL ASSISTANT (MVA) AGREEMENT
This Agreement (the "Agreement") is made as of [insert date here] (the "Effective Date") by and between [insert your company name here], a [state company incorporated and/ or company structure type, e.g., California sole proprietorship], with a principal place of business at [insert address here] ("the Company"), and _____
_____, a(n) individual/corporation/limited liability company residing at
_____("the MVA").

Scope of the Services
During the term of this Agreement, starting on the Effective Date, the services to be performed by MVA will consist of a series of discrete, mutually agreed-upon projects listed in Exhibit A. As new projects are agreed to, new exhibits may be added to this Agreement. Deliverables associated with each project will be as mutually determined by the parties. MVA will provide such services in a professional manner.

Compensation
As compensation in full for the services to be performed on behalf of the Company under this Agreement, and for the other obligations of MVA arising hereunder, the Company

---

figure 4.3–Sample MVA contract

will pay MVA according to the schedule set forth at Exhibit A ("the Consulting Fee"). The Consulting Fee shall constitute the MVA's sole compensation for the performance of the MVA's services under this Agreement. The Company may offset any amount payable hereunder against any payments due from the MVA pursuant to any other written agreement or arrangement.

Performance

MVA is required to meet all quality of work and reasonable completion schedules set forth by the Company. Completion schedules are to be set forth in such a way that they can reasonably be expected to be completed during normal business hours.

Inventions

MVA assigns to the Company, without further consideration, all right, title, and interest (throughout the United States and in all foreign countries), free and clear of all liens and encumbrances, in and to all inventions. The inventions shall be the sole property of the Company, whether or not copyrightable or patentable. MVA agrees to maintain adequate and current written records on the development of all inventions, which shall also remain the sole property of the Company. "Inventions" means all ideas, processes, inventions, technology, designs, formulas, discoveries, patents, copyrights, and trademarks, and all improvements, rights, and claims related to the foregoing, that are conceived, developed, or reduced to practice by MVA alone or with others.

Method of Performing the Services

It is expressly agreed and understood that MVA is performing services under this Agreement as an independent contractor for the Company and MVA is neither an employee nor an agent of the Company. MVA will have sole control over the detailed method of performance of the services, the manner and method of performing same being under the sole control and discretion of MVA , and the Company's only interest being in the results of such services. The Company's liability hereunder will be limited to payment of the compensation provided in this Agreement. MVA acknowledges his/

figure 4.3–Sample MVA contract, continued

her obligation to obtain appropriate insurance coverage for his/her own benefit. Any and all personnel hired by the MVA , as employees, consultants, agents or otherwise (collectively, "Staff"), shall be the responsibility of the MVA. The MVA will be responsible for withholding, accruing and paying all income, social security and other taxes and amounts required by law for the Consulting Fee and all payments to the Staff, if any. The MVA will also be responsible for all statutory insurance and other benefits required by law for the MVA and the Staff and all other benefits promised to the Staff by the MVA, if any. The MVA shall provide the Company with a completed W-9 form.

MVA will have no authority to act, to make any representation, to enter into any contract or commitment or to incur any liability on behalf of the Company.

Proprietary Rights and Confidentiality

MVA will not at any time or in any manner, either directly or indirectly, use for the personal benefit, or divulge, disclose, or communicate in any manner, any information that is proprietary to [your company name here]. MVA will protect such information and treat it as strictly confidential. This provision will continue to be effective after the termination of this Agreement. Upon termination of this Agreement, MVA will return to [your company name here] all records, notes, documentation, and other items that were used, created, or controlled by "the Company" during the term of this Agreement.

Assignment

MVA may not assign to or subcontract with any person or entity, this Agreement or any right or obligation hereunder without the Company's written consent. [Your company name here] may assign this Agreement to any parent or subsidiary company.

Termination

Either party may terminate this Agreement at any time upon written notice to the other party. Upon the termination of this Agreement for whatever reason: a) all obligations of the parties hereunder shall cease; b) [your company name here] shall pay the MVA all

figure 4.3–Sample MVA contract, continued

Consulting Fees due up to the date of such termination; and (c) the Contractor shall return to [your company name here] all confidential information.

Indemnification

Contractor will defend, indemnify, and hold harmless [your company name here], its officers, directors, and employees against all liability, loss, cost, or expense associated with any claims, suits, actions, or demands of any nature and description by reason of damage or injury (including death) to any person or property caused by MVA's negligence, breach of this Agreement, or performance of services hereunder.

Modification

No modification or waiver of this Agreement shall be binding unless in writing and signed by the parties hereto.

Waiver

The waiver by either party of any breach by the other party of any of its obligations hereunder or the failure of such party to exercise any of its rights in respect of such breach shall not be deemed to be a waiver of any subsequent breach.

Arbitration

Any action to enforce or interpret this Agreement or to resolve disputes between [your company name here] and the MVA by, or against any party, shall be settled by arbitration in accordance with the rules of the American Arbitration Association. Arbitration shall be the exclusive dispute resolution process in the [state in which you or your company do business or is incorporated]. Any party may commence arbitration by sending a written demand for arbitration to the other parties. Such demand shall set forth the nature of the matter to be resolved by arbitration. Arbitration shall be conducted at [city of state in which American Arbitration Association office is located], [state in which American Arbitration Association office is located]. The substantive law of the State of [state in which arbitration is to occur] shall be applied by the arbitrator to the resolution of the

figure 4.3–Sample MVA contract, continued

dispute. The parties shall share equally all initial costs of arbitration. The prevailing party shall be entitled to reimbursement of attorney fees, costs, and expenses incurred in connection with the arbitration. All decisions of the arbitrator shall be final, binding, and conclusive on all parties. Judgment may be entered upon any such decision in accordance with applicable law in any court having jurisdiction thereof.

Governing Law

This Agreement will be governed by and construed in accordance with the laws of the State of [state in which your business will seek arbitration].

IN WITNESS WHEREOF, the parties hereto have executed this Agreement as of the date set forth above.

_____
NAME

_____
NAME

Initial _____

figure 4.3–Sample MVA contract, continued

Exhibit A

COMPENSATION

Month ONE:

Month TWO:

Month THREE:

Month FOUR and ongoing:

Invoices must be submitted monthly in order to receive compensation. Payment terms are net 10 days. [Your company name here] will not reimburse the MVA for normal and customary business expenses, including, but not limited to, the full cost of all authorized travel, lodging, and meal expenses for out-of-town trips, expenses relating to entertainment of clients, prospective clients, and media, unless otherwise agreed upon in writing.

Scope of the Project. Public relations campaign for [your company name here]; additional duties will be added on full time agreement for [your company name here].

Roles and Responsibilities. Including but not limited to providing media list database research and building, creating pitches, pitching A-list media, calling, following up, getting placement, print features, interviews on radio and television. Pitching television show concepts and appearances.

figure 4.3–Sample MVA contract, continued

WIPEOUT

I can't seem to get my systems organized for online marketing. There's too much to do, not enough time in the day. How can I get my social networking done without taking away from other important tasks that need attention?

WAVE TIP

You do not need to be social online 24/7. Just set a time every day to interact online and a plan as to which sites you want to interact on. When you are first setting up your social presence, it will definitely take a bit more time (on average 15 to 25 hours per week), but once you are set within the first 3 months, it shouldn't take more than an hour a day (unless you have decided to use social sites as your customer service center). Get organized by using social media dashboards such as Hootsuite or Tweetdeck so that you can post and track from one central location.

KNOW THE TIDE

find out where your customers are posting online and
use online social sites as your customer service portal

*Customer service is
the new marketing.*
—AMY COSPER,
EDITOR-IN-CHIEF,
ENTREPRENEUR MAGAZINE

With all of the tracking systems that
the government has in place as well as
those the new technologies offer, finding out what your markets'
buying behaviors are is a lot easier today compared to even a year
ago, let alone five years ago. One of the most interesting studies is
one conducted by 15miles, an SEO and internet marketing company,
in partnership with comScore, a digital data survey company. They
observed online behavior through a survey of more than 4,000 local
business owners. More than 70 percent said they go online first for
local business information. The study also reported that 69 percent
of consumers are more likely to buy from a local business if its
information is available on a social network. For the complete study,
check out updates at www.localsearchstudy.com/. What is amazing
about this study is how the shift to online has also influenced buying
behaviors, with a majority of consumers going online to do business

first. There is every sign that this number will continue to increase substantially, and quickly, as businesses start to jump online due to constant customer demand.

Studying your market's online behaviors

A hidden gem that can help compile online and demographic buying behaviors is the Small Business Development Center (SBDC). You can locate the office nearest your business through www.sba.gov. I have also found that the SBDC will help you with international marketing information, and they have additional resources in this area. If you can't find an office near you, jump online and go for a simple Google or Bing visit with keywords about your market. This is another way to obtain buying behaviors as well.

> Use the advanced search option at search.twitter.com by using keywords to look up conversations that your focus market is having about you or your competition.

In addition to finding out buying behaviors, you need to know where your focus market hangs out and posts online. What works for one industry or group of people might not work for the next. You need to find out which digital communities they belong to. If you aren't sure, ask them! Your customers know which sites they frequent online. They know where they share content, where they post the most, and what blogs they read daily. You can offer incentives to get them to share this information with you—free downloads, coupons, or exposure/a link on your blog. The more you can identify where your focus market is hanging out, the better you can create content specifically for them to bring them back into your business. Knowing where your customers are online is the first step in being able to market to them.

Use advanced search functions on social sites

You are probably thinking that finding your future customers and clients online is a really, really hard process. Right? Wrong. Actually, it is just like going to the grocery store and picking items off a shelf. So, let's do this. Let's go shopping online for customers. Oh this is going to be fun! Let's go to the Twitter store first, at search.twitter.com to visit the advanced search section. Once you get there, just say (in this case, type) exactly what you want by using keywords that describe your customer and/or use key "needs" words that they would use to find you. This could be "women in business," "at-home moms," "chefs," or "wine connoisseurs." For the type and the needs words it could be: "looking for organization," "need a break," "want new ingredients," or "this wine is good." Then click on search, and woo hoo! There they are. Your customers are talking about you, to you, or for you. Now, bring them home by following them on Twitter.

Next, let's pay a visit to the Facebook shopping center. This one has a huge selection of customers, so let's get right in there. Starting with the search section, choose from those same keywords that you used at the Twitter market, and type them in. When the window pops up with fan pages and groups that have those keywords in them, you can certainly browse those sections, join a few groups, like a few fan pages, and start engaging with them. You can also keep on shopping and click on the option that says "See more results," all the way at the bottom of the pop-up. Once you click on that, more fan pages and groups pop up. However, you want to go into the "Posts by Everyone" section on the left toolbar. (At least that is where it was at the time this was written. If it is not, please visit the blog for this book to get the most recent information at www.socialwavebook.com.) Now, those posts by everyone that pop up include all the people on Facebook using those keywords or that have those keywords in their profiles. There you have it, instant waves.

Last but not least, let's go to LinkedIn and shop in its advanced section on the upper right search box. Once you click on the advanced option, a new page will pop up somewhat like on Twitter. It has a ton of different search options that you can use with your keywords to go on a shopping spree. You can look customers up by industry, relationship level, how long they have been on LinkedIn, what their level is at the company they work for, their language, years of experience, and so much more. I say shop 'til you drop!

Set up your customer service portal online

Here we are, it is now time to focus on your customer service. Now that you have gone shopping for new customers and are aware of all of the social media vehicles available online, you need to get serious and use online social sites as customer service portals for your brand. Live chat options on websites and blogs are becoming more popular, but those are great only once people are on your site. What about the prospects or customers who have not yet made it to your site? Once you locate where your market is online, and where, exactly, they are posting, set up a social account on the applicable site(s) and, as mentioned earlier in the book, post the times you are available to answer questions or chat live via those social sites. You can always direct them to your site or customer service line for offline hours.

An excellent example of how a business set up and utilized a customer service portal online is Eurail.com, an e-commerce site for Eurail train passes. When Mashable.com, a social media news site that honored Eurail with the "Best Social Media Customer Service" category award, asked what makes Eurail's social media customer service so great, Chantal Sukel, the campaign manager for Eurail.com, replied, "Eurail.com is lucky enough to have extremely dedicated agents that strive to answer all questions within eight hours or sooner. Not only in English, but also Spanish and even Dutch or German. Our fans receive a personal reply, not a script. They talk to an actual human being who can give them anecdotes and tips from their own rail travel experiences." The point to this example is: Let your team members be the human beings they are. This is an excellent approach with customer service online that many corporations and small businesses would do well to embrace. Empowering your team empowers the customer and the brand. Kudos to Eurail.com for getting it and doing it, and to Mashable. com for acknowledging them.

It's a good idea to have your support team end their emails with, "Did you like our customer service today? We would love to hear about it via [your Twitter account] on Twitter or www.facebook.com/[your Facebook address]." This is a great way to get feedback on your online customer service as well as add activity to your newsfeeds and exposure about and for your brand. Just by planting this seed in the emails, it prompts the customer to think about taking action and writing about you. Often customers do not think about sharing a good or great experience; they tend to want to focus on the yucky ones. This will encourage them to get online, get active, and share their experience. Again, remember that people in general love to be heard. In this quest for acknowledgement, it helps increase positive awareness for your brand. That is a win-win situation..

Managing your newsfeeds

Newsfeeds can mean a few different things, so let's clarify it before we motor into deeper marketing waters. A web feed (or newsfeed) is for providing users on a particular site, such as Facebook or Twitter, frequently updated content by and from their connections—for example, status updates. Another type of feed is an RSS feed. (No, it is not something you eat!) RSS stands for real simple syndication, or a syndicated web feed allowing users to subscribe to it. This is how people can subscribe to your blog so they can get your posts and updates every time you post them online. Think of your RSS subscribers as magazine subscribers. You can also have a collection of web feeds and have them sent to what is called an aggregator, aka a feed reader. Phew, did that all make sense? If not, check out some more newsfeed stuff at www.socialwavebook.com.

Now let's talk about status updates. It is extremely important when you sign in on your social sites that you immediately update your status with a either a quick post, a question (be careful what you ask, and make sure you really want to know the answer), or motivational or humorous quotes. This keeps your profile active and shows you are online engaging, which is key in building quality connections and engaging online. These updates shouldn't take more than 30 seconds to post after you sign in. Go on to either your social media dashboard (Hootsuite, Tweetdeck) and do a status update out to all of the sites you are active on, or go to each site and post. Take no more than 10 minutes to do this. A quick, simple, effective post is called a "bizper post," one where you include a balance of personal and business update. It is important to add a personal approach to your posts and status updates every so often. At the same time, don't just make it personal without inserting a quick business seed. Bizper post means "biz" for "business" and "per" for "personal." Some bizper post examples are:

- I am sitting at Starbucks, sipping a mocha—working on my presentation for Microsoft
- Off to watch a movie before I work on my new makeup line launch
- Baking cookies for the kiddos (snuck one in for me), then off to work on speaking presentation for Intuit
- Soccer practice with kids, sitting on the sideline brainstorming ideas for new leadership coaching program

After you have posted your own status update, skip on over to the newsfeed to stay as informed as you can on what your connections are doing, saying, and where they are going online—without getting overwhelmed. The best way to do this and still have time to eat and sleep is perform a 3/2 newsfeed check. After you sign in and update your status, do a quick once-over on the newsfeed for the site you are on. Choose no more and no less than 3 posts or people to respond to, and spend no more than 2 minutes to respond or add to the post. This helps you engage with people online. They will know that it is not all about you posting your status updates online, that you actually read the feeds, and care enough to post a comment back to them about something they said. They, of course, feel heard and more trust builds. Whatever you do, do not sales bitch, post a link to your fan page or website, etc.— unless they specifically ask for it in a reply. Remember, when you are responding, you are just adding to the conversation.

As much as you would like to think that you do not care what people are eating, doing, or saying, studies show that actually you do. You care at a deeper level because this is how you relate to others—by having something in common. So whether someone posts about ice skating, and you just happen to have a passion for it, or someone posts about their favorite tea drink that you enjoy, as long as you can relate to having it in common, the connection will begin right then and there. The same rings true when you post. What do you think is the meaning of people "liking" your posts and thoughts on Facebook? They are basically saying that they can relate to you. So don't fight reading about what your neighbor Sue Smith had for breakfast. If you like bacon and eggs and she reported having them, you might just find yourself with a new breakfast buddy in time. That's not to say you need to become best friends with your neighbor just because you happen to like the same thing for breakfast; it's just that the in-common is what relationships are built on. So do not be afraid to post what you like to eat, what you had to eat, or what you are doing. Just keep it clean.

> **Quick time management tip**: When connections respond to something that you posted online with a thank you, there is no need to thank them for thanking you. Just put the mouse down and back away from the post.

Connecting with high-level networkers online

A majority of the opportunities that you can come across on a daily basis are generated by your high-level networkers (HLN). HLNs are active online, have at least 500 connections, and have powerful profiles, meaning their profile information is complete. They have also taken the time to custom design their profiles and set up what are called vanity urls for each site. For example, my vanity URL for my Facebook fan page is www.facebook.com/starrhalldotcom, and for my personal Facebook page it is www.facebook.com/starrhall. For LinkedIn, it is www.Linekdin/in/starrhall, for Twitter- www.twitter.com/starrhall, and for my YouTube channel it is www.youtube.com/starrhalldotcom. By fixing your social sites to become vanity URLs geared to your branding, you not only simplify it in your market's mind, you also add power to your brand. On the flip side, if you keep your social URLs like www.facebook.com/13728934/eth/9348, where is the power branding in that? Maybe you are doing a great branding job for Facebook, but wait, they don't pay you to brand them. At least get your brand name in there, which, by the way, brings us to another point. Do you still have yourname@aol.com for your email address? Or suzyQ_546464@yahoo.com? That's like insisting on branding AOL or Yahoo! and definitely irritating your customers by making them remember a bunch of numbers in your email. By the time they go online to email you and request information, once they get to the underscore in your email, they have completely forgotten why they were emailing you in the first place! Change your emails (all of them) to your brand name, and please keep out the dashes, numbers, and underscores. My email is quite simple—starr@starrhall.com. You could be in the middle of nowhere with your car broken down and email me from your blackberry just off of memory. See how easy that is? However, if you try to remember AAA's email, um, forget it. You have a better chance emailing me to come and get you. OK, you get the point. Brand yourself, not someone that isn't paying you to brand them.

Because you want to become an HLN, take a few minutes to set your URLs at the following sites:

- *LinkedIn.* Go to your profile and find the line that says "Public Profile." Click on the edit option right next to it, and set your URL name.
- *Twitter.* Just go to your profile under "Settings" and set your username. Our username extension, for example www.twitter.com/starrhall, the Starr Hall is my username/extension.

- *Facebook*. www.facebook.com/username.
- *YouTube*. This is done during the set-up phase, or go to your "channel" and edit the URL link.
- *StumbleUpon*. Currently you can only customize your username. StumbleUpon will not let you change it more than once, so choose wisely.

When looking for HLN to add to your center of influence, broaden your search beyond the obvious and the immediate. Consider business executives, business owners, bankers, venture capitalists, insurance brokers, consultants, and other professionals who meet the following criteria:

1. They have regular contact with the types of individuals who fit the profile of your ideal client.
2. They are trusted and respected by you and by others. If you do not yet know them, check out their recommendations, awards, and accolades.
3. They are connectors, meaning they seem like they would be willing to provide you with referrals or introductions should the opportunity arise. People that hide their connections or keep them confidential might not be the best connectors online. Still, you can always ask them. If they kindly and professionally answer that they would be more than willing to connect you with anyone in their center, but they keep their contacts confidential for competition reasons, then by all means move full speed ahead and connect away. Also let them know that you will obviously do the same. As soon as they connect with you, ask them if there is anyone in a particular profession that they are actively seeking to connect with. Let them know that you will look through your contacts or give them full permission to browse your connections and let you know if there is anyone that piques their interest. Make the introduction happen, and always close the introduction with, "Please keep me informed

on the outcome." This way you will know when your referral introductions turn to business for someone else.

Finding target market connections online

Before we dig into finding your target market connections (TMC) online, let's examine the difference between an HLN and a TMC. HLNs are connectors. They will either do a higher level of business with you or refer you to people that will. They are mostly leaders. TMC are more like online seekers. They are looking for you or your product or service by posting in groups and discussions. TMC are more product, rather than service, seekers. HLN are service and consulting seekers. To find your target market, you need to search with keywords on social sites, describe your target market with keywords, for example, *marketing manager, director, CEO, executive, sales, customer service, speaking, meeting planner*, etc.

Not to confuse you here, but HLN could use the same keywords for their search. Let me break it down for you:

1. High-Level Networkers (HLN):
   - Are active online, leading discussions
   - Have at least 500 connections per profile
   - Have powerful profiles
2. Target Market Connections (TMC) are:
   - Mostly seekers online
   - In groups and discussion areas of same topic/interest
   - Responding rather than leading discussions and posts.

> Although helpful in building trust more quickly, the scripts for Twitter, YouTube, and StumbleUpon are not necessary. Instead, you can simply click "follow" on Twitter and StumbleUpon, or click "subscribe" or "add as friend" on YouTube.

Now that you are finding these types of focus market connections online, what do you do with them? You need to reach out to them and/or send them an invite to connect. When you send an invite to connect with someone that you do not know, adapt the script in

Hello [insert name here],

I am a high-level networker and I would like to add you to my LinkedIn network. If you are not an open networker, please do not report this as spam; simply archive or delete my email.

Thank you for your time and consideration.

Kindly,

[insert name here]

[insert title here]

figure 5.1–LinkedIn invitation script

Figure 5.1 and send it as an email invite. Make sure that you add your own personality. Use this script as a guideline.

LinkedIn currently does not allow you to add your website in invite emails, and a character limit might apply, which might necessitate editing the script in Figure 5.1.

You can also ask for introductions through people to whom you are already connected and know on LinkedIn, or reach out to them via groups that they are already involved in.

Making connections on Facebook with HLNs

Facebook is a bit different when it comes to how you can and should be reaching out to connect on this site. You can certainly send an invite to connect with a personal message or use the script included in this section. You cannot invite someone by posting on their wall or fan page unless you are connected with them. Remember anything that you post on someone's wall is not private, all of their connections will be able to read it. If the person's profile has privacy settings set to not allow postings on their wall or fan page, a message will pop up on your screen to let you know you cannot post on that wall.

Hello [insert name here],

I am expanding my professional network on Facebook, and I would love to connect with you online, however, if you are not an open networker, no worries, simply delete or ignore my invite. Otherwise, I look forward to getting to know you on Facebook.

Thank you for your time and consideration.

Kindly, [insert name here]

[insert title and/or website here]

figure 5.2–Facebook invitation script

Adapt the script in Figure 5.2 to reach out to Facebook networkers through the Facebook message system.

Twitter

Go to each site and navigate. Check out "Who to Follow" section in the navigation bar on Twitter "to build a following." You can also search on Twitter by browsing interests via category in this same section. Check this at least once per week while you are building your connections.

If you already know the person online but are not yet connected via the web, try the script in Figure 5.3 on page 91.

Finding new connections on Facebook or LinkedIn
Add suggested friends located on your homepage. Check once per week. If you do not know them, do a picture and profile check before you extend an invite. Make sure they are professional HLN or TMC, or get to know them through a mutual group.

Twitter is different from other social media because all you do is follow someone—you don't need their permission to connect. However if they aren't following you and you want them to, you need to give them a reason. Try posting something that just says:

If you want someone to follow you back, tweet them with their username in the tweet and mention something you like about their site, business, or product.

This will show them that you have taken the time to get to know them and in return they are most likely to do the same. If they don't respond from that tweet, wait a few days and send another that says:

I thought you might be interested in (and then include a link to something that relates to their business, personality, or product).

figure 5.3–Twitter invitation script

A few bonus steps on how to find new connections or people you know on Twitter are:

- Find them on other networks or invite them by sending email via Twitter, Gmail, Yahoo!, AOL, Hotmail, or MSN.
- Visit Twitaholic.com. These are people that are followed the most on Twitter, which means they are HLN!
- Go to http://tweetadder.com/download to download the Tweet Adder program, which allows you to set it at a certain amount of new followings per day or week. It does have a free trial. However, it will ask you to upgrade for a fee at a later date. Although this is one of the better auto-follow softwares, be careful with auto-follow as you do not want just anyone following you, and vice versa. These programs are getting better at allowing you to find people via keywords and regions.

- At Twitter Grader, http://twittergrader.com/location, you'll find top Tweeters by location!
- Go to twitterlocal.net to find local businesses and TMC using the TwitterLocal application.

WIPEOUT

How do I know what keywords to look up on these social sites so that I can find my target market online?

WAVE TIP

There are several powerful sites that can help you determine what the right keywords are for your target market. Wordtracker.com or keywordpoint.com (both have free trials) also allow you to look up what keywords people are using to find you through your Google Analytics that you set up on your site. You did set it up right? If not, do that right now!

6

HOW TO DEAL WITH THE SHARKS ONLINE

a complete overview on how to deal with negative posts, people, and online trolling (also known as cranky people)

> *Before you begin on the journey of revenge, dig two graves.*
>
> —PROVERB

As you grow your presence online, post more, interact more, ask questions, and answer questions, you are more than likely going to come across a few mean people, or trolls. Trolls can sometimes differ from just plain old cranks. In internet slang, a troll is someone who posts inflammatory, extraneous, or off-topic messages in an online community such as a discussion forum, chat room, or blog, with the primary intent of provoking other users into an emotional response, or of otherwise disrupting the normal on-topic discussion. On the other hand, cranks, or mean people, will just post mean things about you, your product or service, or the experience they had with you.

Dealing with trolls and mean people

The approach you should take when dealing with any negative posts or outreach online has an easy-to-remember acronym. It's the ARM response, which guides you to:

A: Acknowledge the pain
R: Respond politely
M: Make it right

The last step might not apply to trolling. Sometimes the best thing to do with some trolls is to acknowledge, post politely once, and leave it alone.

There are endless numbers of sites and online resources that people can use now to write reviews, rant, complain, and start petitions. Groubal is a site that claims to champion consumer complaints by taking popular petitions to corporations and business and demanding answers. It has set up a viral approach by gathering signatures from upset customers that are or have experienced the problem or just from people that support the complaint cause. Sites like these will continue to get more traction as more of them surface. Some general service review sites are Yelp, TripAdvisor, and Angie's List; a few product sites to check out are Buzzillions.com and epinions.com. Go ahead and set this book down for a few minutes so you can check yourself out on these review sites. Do this periodically, and get ready to implement the ARM response as needed.

Recently a client called over the weekend because someone had a terrible experience at her store. I walked her through the ARM response and then followed the situation over the next few days. Sure enough, she won over a very upset customer who is even willing to try her place again. The negative post was even removed. (By the way, do not get your hopes up on that one or request it. If they remove, it great; if not, then just let it go.)

Take a quick 30 minutes to put your ARM response plan in place, and communicate it with your team. If you are a one-person show, then communicate it to your trusted family and friends. Always be prepared to take action when dealing with cranks or trolls, but do take at least an hour after a yucky post or review (no more than 24 hours) to vent offline, punch a pillow, go to a mountain top and scream, or go sing as loud as you can in your car just to get the steam off. Once you can respond from a place of peace, and not from a place of anger, then you can ARM away.

Get off the stream

When you post using the ARM response, make sure that you post only once in response to a negative post. There is no need to go back and forth with someone who is upset. As long as you acknowledged, responded politely, and tried to make it right, that is all you need to do. The more posting that you do back and forth, the more likely that post is to rise higher in the search engines and stay there longer. Furthermore, you are just adding fuel to the fire.

Nestlé regretted its actions and posts shortly after its response to a few negative posts on its fan page by Greenpeace and like-minded individuals over its policy of buying palm oil. Greenpeace accused Nestlé of supporting deforestation and threatening the orangutan monkeys with extinction. Greenpeace created a video that likened eating a Kit Kat bar to killing an Orangutan. That video was placed on YouTube and has received millions of views to date. Nestlé's response to this upset group of people was to have the video removed, which only angered the Greenpeace members. Nestlé claimed the video violated its trademark. That was most likely true, but the removal angered Greenpeace so much that it organized its members to start making comments on the Nestlé Facebook page. Nestlé then moved to protect its Facebook page by removing critical comments and removing comments where the user had changed its profile picture to one of the altered Nestlé logo. This move by Nestlé angered Greenpeace even more and caused its supporters to flock to the Nestlé page and post more negative comments and more images of the altered logo. Continuing to do the same thing and expecting the results to change, Nestlé continued to remove comments with the altered logo from its Facebook page until it could no longer keep up with the posts. At that point, Nestlé proudly announced its intention to use only sustainable palm oil by—wait for it—2015! To this day, the search engines still house thousands of these posts.

Humanize your brand

With the big corporations and businesses growing so fast that they don't even know who is answering their phones anymore, now is the time to get back to being a human brand. People want to connect with a person, not a corporation. For the most part, cranky people do not seem to attack a humanized brand as much as a front brand, and you can humanize your brand by adding a personal touch to your messaging, perhaps a photo, also known as an "avatar," that is, the graphical representation of the user or the user's alter ego or character. Kira Wampler, who handled the Intuit Small Business community, said in an interview that engaging and displaying human avatars changed sentiment from 65 percent negative towards QuickBooks to only 35 percent negative. "My avatar was always a picture of one of my children and me during that time. I regularly told folks that it was easy to say [screw you] to Intuit, the brand, but really hard to swear at the mommy and the baby. Especially when the mommy was helping," says Kira.

Performing intentional acts of kindness is another way that a brand can add a more human persona to its image. A humanized brand has "trust agents," people who have trust written all over their picture. This trust is apparent by and in its actions. According a report compiled by tendwatching.com published in the December 29, 2010, Center for Media Research's brief, the number-one consumer trend for 2011 is a craving "for realness, for the human touch." Take the opportunities created by social marketing and perform random yet intentional acts of kindness. Follow your clients or customers on Twitter, and react to their real time updates. Did someone just Tweet that they enjoy coffee? Send him a Starbucks gift card. Did someone just tweet about her birthday? Send a card or a Groupon coupon! Let your customers know you're listening.

Because you should always track your results, include a coupon with a specific promotional code for your own services along with a gift or arrangement. This way you'll know if the gift enticed the customer to go on to purchase more from you.

Recently, I received a flower delivery on Valentines' Day with a card that said, "We love you! We would have Tweeted out our love for you, but we couldn't say it in just 140 characters. Please visit this website to find out who this is from." When I went to the website, there was a personal video greeting from my email software company telling me how much they appreciated and loved my businesses. They then took it even further and asked me to pay it forward and enter the name and address of someone to whom I would like them to send a $50 restaurant gift card. Not only did they humanize their brand by this amazing act of kindness, they asked me to pay it forward and they got a new lead from me as well. Brilliant on all levels!

Have a damage control plan in place

No matter how proactive you are and how strong your brand position is in the marketplace, customers will start to question your brand when they read or hear about problems. And if there is an information void, those customers tend to fill in the gaps with their own thoughts on what the cause may be. That's why it is important to respond to issues quickly, even if the message is just "We're looking into it." Communication is key when cleaning up damage online or off. Equally important, make sure that every employee knows the same message all the way down the chain of command. And when that message changes, don't forget to communicate those changes. This serves two purposes: It gives the public a sense that you have your arms around the issue, and it gives your employees a sense of unity, a sense that they are working together to solve a common problem.

With the online world now moving at the speed of light, it is also important to have a team of trusted employees or representatives who are willing to be available on a moment's notice and work round the clock to help you evaluate the situation and respond. Before you respond, however, you need to assess the situation online by utilizing tools that are publicly available, such as online search engines, Twitter Search, newsfeeds, and WhosTalkin.com. Watch the "attacker's" website or blog as well. He may change his tune or consumers may react negatively and post comments about his comment on their site. Take some time to monitor the volume of response and the type of consumer reaction. Is it growing or falling off? Is it supportive or negative? Is it changing over time? By identifying what your focus audience's reaction is, you can then format a response. Remember, your response could validate that there is an issue and may further perpetuate a negative situation. Avoid responding too quickly, using a tone that is "brand corporate," or issuing a one-way-only media release posted on your website or blog. These approaches are typically not well-received in the social media arena.

WIPEOUT

Someone recently posted a negative review about my company online, what should I do?

WAVE TIP

Whatever you do, do not ignore it, reach out to the person on that site and make it right, as well as let them know you understand (even if you don't!). If the site does not allow you to post or reply and you cannot reach out to them directly, you might publish a blog post about it to include the top three ways that you would make it right. This puts you in the power seat, helps your brand reputation, and shows that you are proactive as well as care about what people think and say about you.

7

JUMPING ON THE BLOGGING BOAT

how to connect with your focus market
through the power of blogging

> *A blog is merely a tool that lets you do anything from change the world to share your shopping list.*
> —Unknown

The first thing you need to decide when you build your blog is what you want to accomplish with it, and what it can do if successful. Blogs can be extremely powerful not only in getting a message out there but also in continuing a conversation and building relationships with prospects and customers. In the most basic terms, blogging is about being yourself and posting the unedited you. OK, let's qualify that a little last point a bit; "unedited" still means within good taste, unless your brand personality is more brash or edgy. Then, by all means forget the taste and post away.

The premier blog platforms

Although WordPress still seems to be the leading blog platform of choice, Tumblr is a strong second contender. In several articles and surveys released on Mashable.com, a social media news site, Tumblr has often come in close to last, but this blog platform can't be beat for ease of use. Regardless of others' opinions, you need to determine which platform is best for your brand, and go for it. If you do not yet have a blog set up on your site, or if your site is not based on a blog platform such as WordPress, it is time to take some major action here.

WordPress is a free blogging platform that offers the largest amount of flexibility. Yes, it is a bit more technical than most other blogging platforms, so novice users might find it tricky to get started. But with that said, you can have zero html understanding or blog platform knowledge and be up to speed with your WordPress blog. Once you get started, you can easily use its many user-friendly features to create a great blog.

Tumblr is a more lightweight blogging system. You can upload a variety of multimedia such as text, images, quotes, links, chat, music, and videos. You can follow other users on Tumblr and see their posts. If they become friends with you, they can also see your posts. You can easily tumble their blog post onto your blog and vice versa. Tumblr is split into four main subpages: Dashboard, Popular, Goodies, and Account.

Posterous is another blog platform worth exploring. It has been rated one of the easiest and fastest blog platforms to use. You can send it your content, graphics, videos, and other files, and it will create a blog for you at no addition charge. Although its designs are professional compared to some of the other platforms, they are still limited.

No matter which blog platform you choose, just make sure that you take the time to watch one of the demo videos so you have an understanding of how it works and how it can benefit your brand online. Once you have decided on the platform that is right for you, get it set up so you can start blogging and utilizing the tips and strategies in this book. There is no time to waste here. There is blogging to be done!

Key benefits of blogging

Business startups often need to build their credibility quickly to compete with established competition. By positioning yourself as an expert in your field through your blog, you can attract media attention and serve as a quoted source in published articles and on other blog sites, which will help you gain exposure to other markets as well as massive numbers of new leads. As you gain coverage and a following on your blog, you will find that people begin to ask you for interviews and quotes, and professional associations may ask you to give speeches or participate in panel discussions, thus solidifying your credibility. Each time people read your company name and associate it with something positive, it will reinforce their awareness of your brand and help them differentiate your company from your competitors.

Blogs can also help you build stronger relationships by providing quality content and engaging conversations on your blog, as well as by helping you build quality online relationships that can often convince a newcomer to come back and read more or, yes, even buy. By aligning your blog with the goal of attracting repeat business, you can build consumer confidence and trust. For example, by answering posts or having conversations with visitors on your blog, you send a message that you value your clients and share a stake in their success.

A favorite benefit of blogging is partnering with other top bloggers. Doing so helps take you into their markets as well as increase your followers and fans. Your blog can, of course, do the same for a partnering blog. Later in this chapter, you will learn where and how you can reach out to other bloggers to build mutually beneficial relationships.

To help you determine what type of blog you should launch and how often you should post as well as engage, take a few moments to complete the questionnaire in Figure 7.1.

Create your blog message and content

Before we dig into creating content for your blog, there are a few questions to help identify the key message for your blog. Try to be

BLOGGING PLAN QUESTIONNAIRE

Question	Yes	No
1. Do you offer a product?		
2. Do you offer a service?		
3. Is your product or service a top-producing, top-of-mind brand?		
4. Do you feel that your company has been and continues to be properly differentiated among your competitors?		
5. Do you have a strong social media presence on the top four social sites Facebook, Twitter, LinkedIn, and YouTube?		
6. Do you feel that your customer base and market reach is expanding online?		
7. Do you currently have an active online social networking campaign implemented in your marketing strategy?		
8. Do you personally write your own content? (articles, updates, newsletters, etc.)		
9. Do you openly share your industry tips, secrets, and best practices with customers or clients?		
10. Do you consistently communicate with your customers and your target market a minimum of once every 20 days?		

Scoring

Give yourself 2 points for every "no," 4 points for "yes."

20–28 points: You have a few marketing gaps with your brand. Create a WordPress-based blog and post quality content two to four times per week to begin growing your brand in the right direction. Tips throughout this book will help you boost your blog quality to higher levels.

29–40 points: You have put some strong marketing effort into your current brand. However, to boost it, get started launching either a blog of your choice or posting once or twice per week to expand your brand even more online. Go back and look through the questions you answered "no" to and begin focusing on those areas immediately. Reevaluate your blog every three months to make sure that you are on the right branding track.

figure 7.1–Blogging plan questionnaire

as specific as possible in your responses, and try to avoid general statements like, "I want to offer great customer service," because everyone claims they offer that. It needs to be different and compelling. For example, maybe you offer the only mobile massage service that travels in an electric vehicle. A few quick questions to ask yourself in creating your key blog message are:

- What is the top benefit in regard to my products or services that sets me apart from my competition?
- What is new, just added, or generating good responses from my current customers?

With your top benefit and something new or just added, we will begin to form your blogging message in the rest of this chapter. Now we need to look at your blog offer. We will create top tips around your message in a bit. Sit tight, yet read on.

In order to determine your blog offer from your blog message, let's dig deeper in order to determine what your offer(s) should be. Ask yourself these two key questions:

1. What do you want them to know about your industry or topic?
2. What can you offer them (aka free advice, so leave the sales pitching out of this) to help educate them and connect more with what it is that you do? Take this answer and determine how you can save them time, money, or make their lives or business easier with your products or services.

Let's say your website specializes in gardening because you sell gardening products. You need to clearly identify what it is that you want your readers to get from visiting your blog.

Your blog message is you offer greener, more sustainable environmentally conscious products that are less expensive than the non-green. Your blog offer around this key message (aka benefits):

- *Offer quick gardening tips for what to plant during specific times of the year.* This valuable information saves them time and could ultimately save them money by having fewer dead plants that didn't work out.

- *Create top tips on how they can create an organic garden in one hour or less.* Again, you're offering time-saving information that helps the planet and their health.

Each of these might also generate publicity for your blog as well. We will cover that in the publicity chapter soon, very soon.

Blog content is the essence of your branding and your connection with your target market online as well as with the media. You need to create content and posts that are not only relevant to your topic or industry but are also newsworthy, timely, and fill a need or want for your market. Let's look at the top three types of content:

> **Quick tip on additional blog content**
> Improve education by asking readers to contribute their year round tips in a special section on your blog, or run a contest where visitors can vote on the best tried and tested tips and share their stories.

1. *Top Tips and Articles.* We are pages away from digging into exactly how to create these amazing content pieces.
2. *Paragraph Opinion Posts.* Yep, it is OK to share your opinion online; in fact, with blogging, it is encouraged.
3. *Blog Sharing.* Sharing content that other bloggers have posted out on their blog that compliment your products or services. For example, if you are a fitness trainer, this could be local gyms, nutritionists, vitamin companies, etc.

Identify and reach out to potential blog partners

When it comes to blog sharing, you need to develop a partner list of blogs/bloggers with which you would like to build relationships. These relationships are key to getting your blog noticed on other top blogs, as well as to reaching out to new markets and new prospects. A great way to locate top blogs is on Technorati.com, one of the top blog locator sites. You can enter keywords in the search section to locate blogs that you are interested in posting onto your blog or build a relationship with top blogs so in time they will be open to including an interview with you or some of your content on their blog. Another resource for locating top blogs is simply using Google or Bing search. For a blog partner template, visit the website for this book at www.socialwavebook.com.

Once you have your blog ready to go, and your blog partners identified, you need to get the attention of the top bloggers on your list. Although email and posting are great ways to build a relationship with another blogger, sometimes just picking up the phone to let them know you would like to build a relationship is the best way to grab their attention. Why? For the most part, everyone else is posting or emailing them. When calling them, assume that you only have 30 seconds to explain who you are, why you are calling, and the value of your proposed blogging partnerships.

Keeping in touch with blog partners

Even if you have already reached out and talked with the bloggers on your partner list, make sure that you send them an email or post at least once per month to keep your name and blog at top of mind. Don't be buggy, just simply let them know you are there. Be sure to include their posts and content on your site periodically. Share the love, because as we all know, all the world needs is love.

Take time in every single day or week to build relationships with other bloggers and sites online. Create a list of blogs and content sites that you like and feel are relevant to your industry that can compliment what you are already offering. For example, if you are a nutritionist, partnering with gyms, vitamin sites, health blogs, etc. could greatly benefit your site. How? Glad you asked. As you locate sites you like and find content that you want to share with your clients and prospects, include these site links on your blog or throughout your site. These links will help you build search engine ranking with Google and other search engines such as Yahoo! and Bing. In addition, as you begin to

Real World Example	Reporter	"Newsroom, Holly Grant speaking."
	Pitcher	"Good morning Holly, this is Starr Hall calling to suggest a story idea. Can I have 30 seconds of your time?"
	Reporter	"Yes, but no more, can you make it quick?"
	Pitcher	"Sure, Holly, I know you cover the education section here in this community. I teach arts and crafts at the South Side Community Center. We are receiving twice the number of requests and class sign-ups on a new crafting technique called XYZ that we just started to offer here. In fact, we are adding two new teachers, directly as a result of the demand for these classes. Your readers might want to know about this in case they are looking for a hobby for themselves or their children, too."
	Reporter	"That's interesting. I'd like to talk about this when I have more time. How about tomorrow? Can you call back sometime between 10 a.m. and noon?"
	Pitcher	"Sure, I'd be glad to. Thanks for your time."

figure 7.2–"30-second" connection

share these sites, the site owners will pick up that you are linking back to them and start to check you out—and possibly share with their market as well.

It may take you some time to get into the groove and build relationships, which is an ongoing process. Be patient with yourself, and don't put too much pressure on, just continue to take action. Initially you might blog two to three times per week, but as you become busier as a result of all of the business, syndicated columns, and speaking engagements you have drummed up from your online activity and engaging, you may reduce your blog time to once or twice per month. Keep in mind that if you set your foundation, and you persevere, six months down the road you'll started to feel the love and business from your blogging efforts.

Marketing your blog

Marketing your blog is not a one-time effort. You need to consistently reach out and market on a daily or weekly basis in order for your blog to climb the rankings and gain more readers, especially in the beginning. Below are top tips on how you can market your blog.

- *Post out to social sites.* When you create a post on your blog, reach out to your other networks online such as Facebook, LinkedIn, and Twitter to let your fans, followers, and friends know about your recent post. Make sure you include the link back to your blog so all they have to do is click on the link instead of cuting and pasting it. Example: Check out top five tips on social networking at www.insertblogurlhere.com. (Reminder: You can tiny your url by going to bit.ly. If you are using Hootsuite or Tweetdeck, these social media dashboards will automatically tiny the url for you.)

- *Partner with other bloggers.* Words cannot express enough how important it is to reach out to other bloggers online. Bloggers are some of the most approachable and helpful people you can find online. Don't be afraid to reach out to a fellow blogger for help.

- *Include video clips on your blog.* This is a great way not only to connect with your readers on a deeper level when you post them on your blog through sites such as YouTube, but also to pull people over from YouTube to check you out. Videos are quickly becoming one of the top ways to help your blog or site with search engine ranking.

- *Include links.* Another highly effective approach to help raise awareness for your blog is to include links to other blogs, social bookmarking sites, and/or other places where you have been featured online.

- *Monitor mentions and send thank-you posts.* Monitor inbound links, traffic, comments, and mentions of your blog from sites such as Google Alerts (www.google.com/alerts), Technorati, Blogpulse, and Yahoo! Explorer. When you see that your blog has been mentioned or linked back to, send a thank-you and post something sincere directly on that blog in the comment section.

How to monetize your blog

Once you build your site credibility and have some solid site traffic/readers, there are dozens of ways you can monetize your blog. Below are several options to explore once you are ready to make some cash.

- *Advertisements*. Ads come in the form of text links and banner ads. There are many pay-per-click, pay-per-post, and affiliate programs available. There are programs available through Amazon Associates, Google Adsense, and eBay Affiliates, just to name a few.

- *Selling merchandise*. If you do not yet have your own merchandise available for sale, you can use sites such as Cafepress.com to customize hundreds of products with your brand message and/or logo.

- *Industry reviews*. If you are an established expert in your field, this is an excellent way to bring in some revenue from your blog. There are a handful of excellent bloggers out there that review products, events, businesses, and even websites through their blog posts.

- *Donation button*. If your readers love your content and posts, another way to bring in cash flow is by simply asking your readers for donations by adding a donation button to your blog via Paypal. A popular line that has surfaced from bloggers: "If you like this blog, why not buy me a drink or a cup of coffee?"

Consumer reporting on your blog

Let's dig into this one a little deeper to consider adding some flair to your blog: a category or focus on consumer reporting in your industry. This is one of the best ways for bloggers to build readers and engagement. Whether you are new at blogging or have been blogging for a while, reviewing products can be a huge benefit of blogging. Not only do you get to try out new and cool products, you also get a chance to have a company and others know your honest opinion about the products. The keyword here is *honest*. So even if you do not like the product, you need to be transparent about it.

To get the hang of reviewing, you can review products you already own and use. Make a list of product attributes, divide the list into pros and cons, and think deeply about how you use the product in your everyday life, how it helps you, and how you would improve it. Then post your review on your blog.

If there are products you are interested in, search the internet for their PR contacts or look them up on the fabulous LinkedIn. Let them know you are a blogger and you would like to review their products. Include why you would like to do this. There are also sites that can help you get in touch with companies that want bloggers to review their products. Here is a list of just a few.

1. *Buzz Agent* (www.bzzagent.com/) is a favorite site. Not only do you get a chance to review products, but you can also earn points to redeem at MyPoints.
2. *Blogger Linkup* (www.bloggerlinkup.com/) sends you an email several times a week that lists requests for guest bloggers and lists of those who want to guest blog. There are also lists of companies requesting reviews for their products and their contact info.
3. *RepNation* (www.repnation.com/RepNationCom/Home.aspx) allows you to join campaigns, and like Buzz Agent you not only review products but also are rewarded with points to redeem.
4. *Mom Select* (http://momselect.com/index.html) has many opportunities for bloggers. You can pick programs that interest you.
5. *My Blog Spark* (www.myblogspark.com/) provides "sparks" of information directly to its members from some of the best-known consumer brands in the country.

These are just a few sites to get started with. Remember, start out small and work your way up and into consumer reporting. As you get more familiar with blogging and/or reviewing, more opportunities will come along. Don't get frustrated, be patient, and stay focused. Be a voice for your industry. Remember honesty is seen and felt online, so do not try to hide bad products or overdo it with a good review product post—unless you really like those new red stilettos Jessica Simpson just sent you. Then shout it out to the world.

Develop ongoing plan

The key to success with any blog campaign is consistency. You can have the best blog design and content in the world, but without consistency, your efforts will not bear fruit. Some people do not want to take the time to consistently post on their blog and market it, so they choose to hire a VA or blog agency. However, you have made it this far! You can do this successfully on your own if you simply commit to the process. If you are just way too busy, or you have no passion or desire to make this happen, then certainly, outsource. Just make sure your brand personality is all over your blog and with every single post and reply. Create a "lingo chart" for your VAs to use when and as needed. Give them words you use when you write or talk online. Update this list of lingo as your personality changes. Ha, now that was a funny sentence! Hey—change happens!

OK, let's dig deeper to determine who will handle your blog. There are a few options to consider. You can, of course, create your content and posts. Decide right now if you will consistently develop content and post to your blog. Are willing to be consistent for the success of your company? If you absolutely are not committed to this, then you need to outsource your content creation and posts. You can do this by hiring a VA or signing up with your local university's internship program to attract help from students majoring in your field. Students not only love this experience and need it for the good of their future careers, but they also might even do it for school credit/pro-bono, just for the experience. Visit your local university's career center or give it a call to ask how you can post your information for these positions.

Next, you need to decide how often you will post on your blog. Will you be posting daily, weekly, or monthly? If you want to be known as a top blogger in your industry, I suggest you post daily. If you want to have a blog presence and continually build your credibility, I suggest you post several times throughout the week. If you just want to have a blog to post periodically and/or you want to ease yourself into blogging, then post once per month. In order to stay on track, create a content calendar and schedule. Whether you are outsourcing or doing the content and posts yourself, you should have a 6- to12-month blueprint calendar so you have a plan and general idea as to what you will be writing and posting about. You can create this calendar using

WIPEOUT

I have been blogging for a while, now, and I can't seem to get people to read it, let alone post comments or engage, what am I doing wrong and how can I fix it?

WAVE TIP

Consider your blog in light of these two points:

1. How long is the post? If it is more than 750 words, edit it back to 750.
2. Are you asking questions in the post, giving them ways to engage and get involved, or are you just talking one way to them?

If you solicit your readers for suggestions on how to improve your blog in a post, you will encourage more people to engage with your blog. Make sure you list your blog on technorati.com as well as other blog listing directories under your keywords and categories.

the seasons, as with summertime recipes; popular monthly topics in your industry, such as National Women in Business month; or even self-created ones, such as National Eat Your Vegetables Day. I created my own Super Starr Day (notice the two r's?), when we celebrate successes every year, now, on October 22. Yep, that is the success-celebrating day. Oh yeah, and it's also my birthday!

8

THE OCTOPUS APPROACH FOR VIDEO CREATION AND MARKETING

seven steps to creating and marketing your videos online

A s more people use the internet in search of information, online video becomes an increasingly important tool in reaching and connecting with followers, fans, and customers. Video's rise in power as a marketing tool is due to its attractiveness to web surfers. By adding a human smile and a friendly voice, you can build rapport with your customers faster and help them relate to your business on a more personal level.

> *Success seems to be connected with action. Successful people keep moving. They make mistakes, but they don't quit.*
> —CONRAD HILTON

Video is proving to connect customers on a deeper level because it covers and reaches out to all three types of learning styles: the visual where people learn by reading or seeing, the auditory where people connect by listening to audio, and the kinesthetic where people learn and connect best from hands-on methods, which can now be covered in a video via demonstration of a product or service. No matter what industry you are in, your target market includes all three.

Get your video marketing evaluated at www.pixability.com. This site has an excellent tool to analyze your video optimization, Google efforts, and overall video marketing. It will score you in key areas and show you where you need to improve, or what you need to focus on:

OCTOPUS

Offer value,

Call to action,

Tag,

Objections

Pick focus (FAQ, SAQ, on the road, candid camera, bloopers, real you, product demo, story),

Upload,

Short.

In addition to customer connection, videos also help sites show up higher on the search engines. Browsers and search engines are becoming savvier and are spending less time reading endless web pages of text. Instead, they are picking up on keywords tagged on videos appearing on sites.

As a growing business, it is important that you integrate video into your online marketing efforts. Even if you start with a basic video tip on how to best use your product or service, just get it recorded and get it up on YouTube, your own website and/or blog. Although customers like humor and creativity, the message helps them save time or money or makes their life easier, and that is what everyone's looking for.

Key areas of video marketing

There are seven big-picture things you need to keep in mind when creating video marketing pieces. Let's take a look at these key areas in detail:

1. *Offer value.* Every video that you offer needs to include something of value for the viewer, whether it is a tip, resource, or laugh for the day. You don't want to just roll tape for the sake of having video. The following four-video approach is an excellent way to get you started and comfortable with video creation and video marketing. This great technique comes from trafficgeyser.com. (Always give credit, by the way, when you borrow, try, or advise on someone else's techniques. The following is shortened from creating 20 videos to just four at first. Create the four videos as follow:

   - *Two FAQ (Frequently Asked Questions).* These are questions that are frequently asked by your customers or clients. For example, as a fitness trainer, you might video record an answer to "What are the best ways to prepare for a marathon"? (Hint: these can come from your top tips video footage that you are just about to create.)
   - *Two SAQ (Should Ask Questions).* These are questions that your customers or clients should be asking but aren't. This is additional valuable information that will make their lives easier or save them time or money.

2. *Call to action.* Include a call to action in your video. So many websites have great videos and yet no call to action. If you want clients to call you or click on a link, then ask them to. You can also ask them to sign up for your email list or visit your blog. If your video is focused on what's in it for them, then you'll have their undivided attention, so take maximum advantage of this and get them to take the action you want them to take!

3. *Tag.* Use keywords in the video titles as well as the description because search engines will find it much easier to index your video file. Make sure that you include your URL at the end of your video, or go for it and add your URL throughout your video. It is a great way to get additional exposure online. Make sure that your URL copy is in a clearly visible font, and place

it at the bottom middle for better viewing and exposure. Last, name your video correctly and give it a relevant name so it will show up better in search engine results. Your title should be something relevant to what your customer is looking for. For example, if you're selling widgets, then "Mybestwidget. mov" might be a better choice for naming your video than "9077709845wdgt.mov."

4. *Objections*. Address any objections that have surfaced about your products or service. Videos are a great way to respond to upset customers because they can see your face and visually connect that you are sincere. Objections can also be handled by using the FAQ and SAQ approach mentioned in the "Offering Value" section.

5. *Pick a focus*. Whether you choose to create FAQ and SAQ videos, or film on the road, candid camera, bloopers, or even product demos, be creative. Make sure the video has the essence of your brand personality, yet also make sure that the message and/or short story is focused. Do not try to cover 15 things in a 60-second video.

6. *Upload to your site*. Make your videos visible on the first page of your website! Don't hide your marketing on some obscure dark page that an online customer will never find. Including a short video on your homepage can often keep visitors on your site longer. Make sure you keep your video above the fold on your site, meaning they shouldn't have to scroll down to view it.

7. *Shortness is sweet*. Keep your videos short and to the point. Remember, the less people

Tip for your video background
Avoid plain white walls or what's called hospital walls, but minimize distracting backgrounds. If there is a lot going on in your visuals, it will distract from you and your message. It gives people too many other things to look at. It is hard enough keeping people's attention, and if you give them reasons to look elsewhere, they will.

know about you, the shorter their attention span will be when watching your video. Your prospective customers often know little or nothing about you; they simply want to know who you are, what you do, and most importantly, what's in it for them. So give them the message in less than two minutes; often just 60 to 90 seconds can be enough.

Video details

This chapter would not be complete without a few general details about creating and marketing your videos online. These points cover just about everything you will need to know to get going and get some darn good results.

- *Video equipment.* You do not need expensive video equipment; consider using a Flipcam video from Theflip.com. Just pick one up at your local electronics store or online. It is a small camcorder that can shoot a couple of hours of high-definition video, and costs less than $200. It's simple to use and plugs directly into any computer's USB port. It includes easy-to-use editing software to get you up and running quickly. Flip video editing is as easy as color–by-number painting; anyone can do it.

- *Editing software.* If you want more extensive editing software, Camtasia works great on both Macintosh and personal computers. Just make sure that you save your video editing every few minutes, or you might be in tears after an hour of editing. We have all been there, done that! Camtasia ranges from $99 for the Macintosh platform to $399 for the PC. At any price, it is totally worth every penny. You can add subtitles, change the color of type, add in thought bubbles, music, intros, and exits, just to name a few of the program's features. If you just want to record and deliver footage for someone else to edit, reach out to local college students. They work for beer or coffee gift cards and most are extremely tech savvy. Just tell them what message you really want to relay from the footage, and let them have at it. To view a few FAQ and SAQ samples that I did, visit www.socialwavebook.com.

- *Don't worry about being perfect.* You most likely will not like your first take of any video you create. Record a few extra clips to get comfortable in front of the camera, but don't let multiple video takes slow you down to the point of needing weeks or months to create your video. Find the key points to say, rehearse them if you need to, and then speak to the camera, from your heart to your customers. Your confidence will grow as you get happier in front of the camera. Having given that advice, know you can take dozens of takes of your very first video, and yet end up going with video shoot number three!

- *Determine if you want your video to begin playing automatically.* When your customers (or prospective customers) visit your website, do you want your video to play automatically or offer the opportunity to skip your video? Make your choice depending on the behavior of your customers. If you are selling a one-off, and customers will only visit your website once to purchase it, then a video that plays automatically might work just fine. If your customers visit your website multiple times, you may want to consider having your video play on-demand because it could irritate them and make them leave for another website!

- *Be relevant and informative.* Videos that demonstrate step-by-step procedures are great; videos that express an opinion about a specific topic can be useful, too.

- *Create an interesting title for your video.* A good title will grab the attention of users and help sell them on viewing the video. Additionally, the title and description should contain a related keyword-rich phrase relevant to your product, service, or brand to optimize it for SEO.

- *Provide transcripts of your videos.* Search engines love to index HTML, and by surrounding your videos with keyword-rich copy, you can improve the search rank of your video.

- *Create a video sitemap.* For video that is native to your own website, make sure that users and search engine spiders can find your video content. The easiest way to do this is through the use of a video sitemap on your site. Use important keywords in the anchor text links to your videos featured on your video sitemap.
- *Brand your video by adding your logo.* Video is an excellent tool for generating brand awareness for your company or service.
- *Offer the option to embed your video.* Allow other users access to the code that will allow them to embed your video on their website or their blog. Think viral marketing.
- *Allow users to rate your video.* Videos that receive higher ratings from users are the ones that users tend to "favorite" and save.

Sites to upload on

Uploading your video to all of the video site options available can be time consuming. There are paid tools and services you can use to automate uploading of your video to sites on the internet, and there are a few free ones out there as well. These sites, whether Tubemogul. com or TrafficGeyser.com, allow you to upload your video to multiple video sites at the same time. After uploading your video, you can log in to your account with these sites and track the number of views, clicks, or comments on your video. With Tubemogul, you can also track 10 other videos within the system. If you're in a competitive marketplace where video is used a lot, it can be a great advantage to see what other businesses are doing. Note: when it comes to uploading videos on an automated site like TubeMogul, check its most recent upload guidelines because they are constantly changing. Same for YouTube.

Another great video site for marketing is Viddler, which both corporations and individuals can use. Its current tag is "grow your brand with online video." Although it includes some short-story and humorous videos, it is a more business-oriented video site compared to YouTube, which is more focused on entertainment.

If you are looking to upload your FAQ or SAQ, check out Screencast, which allows you to make a video private, public, or hidden with password access. It has free as well as paid-for account options, and even if you have hundreds of training videos, you may find the free accounts sufficient. No matter which video sites you use, make sure you embed the video code, which helps with SEO and improves the look of the video.

Video emailing, conferencing, and live broadcast

There is a super impressive new product at TalkFusion.com. This site offers video emailing with custom templates, video conferencing, and live video broadcasting, as well as the option to publish your videos to over 200 social sites or on its own social video site, the Fusion Wall. Video greetings are and will become a larger part of our online experience because people are desperate to connect outside of copy. Embrace this new vehicle and start feeling it out.

When I launched my first live broadcast using TalkFusion, the recording actually ended up making it to the CEO of TalkFusion. I had a call from him and his team. They were so impressed with my video training webcast recording that they wanted to discuss how we could partner. Isn't it amazing how this online world works? I broadcast a video to my market, it makes it to the CEO of the video broadcast company, and, there you have it- opportunity is born. You never know when it will pop out around the corner from something you posted or something you recorded. Just look at the Justin Bieber story. (I know what you are thinking, is she really going there?). Yes, the Justin craze was born from a YouTube video upload a few years ago. Now he is one of the hottest teenage heart throbs on this planet. I am still trying to figure out what the heck this "Bieber fever" thing is all about. Enlighten me on my blog, please: www.starrhall.com.

As you move forward with your video marketing, make sure that you jump into video emails to and for your clients and customers. They are a great way to say hello as well as use the Octopus approach to take them out online for the masses. Whether you use a video site or you just upload a quick video from your flipcam or webcam, make sure you have some type of analytics tool or system to monitor the success (or sinking) of your video(s). Yes, we are focused on video view success. However, you need to know when your video ship is a-sinkin'—also known as stinkin'. Most video sites automatically have number of views, but check to make sure the analytics, also called "insights," are in place on the video sites you upload to. If you just upload directly to your blog and you do not have this system in place, you will never know if 1 person viewed or 1,000.

While we are talking about videos, let's visit video conferencing. This option is fantastic for jumping online and having a quick group-coaching video session, product demonstration, question-and-answer session, or just visually connecting with people that you meet on social sites. Try hosting one live video conference every month, especially if you have clients around the globe. They love the visual connection as much as you do. It helps you bond and makes your businesses relationship more personable. Always make sure that you are presentable. It's a sorry fact that too many people ignore the professional rule when it comes to videos. Tops that show a lot of bare skin, bright lip stick, torn T-shirts, PJs—those are not allowed on the scene. Behind the scenes, feel free to wear your ducky PJ bottoms with a suit top when doing a live webcast from your home office. Only the cat need know.

Video conferencing sites to check out are Talkfusion.com, iMeet.com, Oovoo.com, and Skype.com. Each site varies as to how many people you can conference with—from two to unlimited.

If you are a speaker or presenter, or have a product demonstration, live video conferences or broadcasts such as those available through Talkfusion, and now Skype, offer screen share options as well as live chat, surveys, and polls. For professional speakers, this has been a great option to use when presenting to groups large and small from the comfort of your own home office. Now as long as you can keep your dogs from barking during your presentations, all is well.

Video optimization

Videos that show up in Google blended search results don't just come from YouTube. Be sure to submit your videos to other quality video sites like Viddler, Vimeo, Metacafe, AOL, MSN, and Yahoo!, to name a few. Again, this all ties into auto-upload of your videos to sites (see page 119), but you can also add an optimization boost by making sure that all of your videos are tagged with keywords in the tagging section as well as the title and the description area.

WIPEOUT

The views on my video are minimal. How can I get more views and promote them to a wider audience other than listing on YouTube?

WAVE TIP

Make sure that your videos are short and to the point. Make sure that you are listing them on multiple directories such as Viddler. You can also use automated video marketing systems like TrafficGeyser.com or TubeMogul.com. You can also add a contest element to your video that can help drive more traffic and push it out virally.

9

SWIMMING IN A SEA OF CONTENT

create compelling content that will set you apart from your competition

> Quality is never
> an accident. It is
> always the result of
> intelligent effort.
> —JOHN RUSKIN

If you could read the thousands of articles, pitches, and top tips that businesses publish on the internet over the years, you'd find that about 90 percent of them on the first round were all sales pitches, businesses boasting at how great they are. Newsflash. This approach in anything, let alone an article or a pitch, does not work on the internet. It is not about you, it is about the reader. The faster you get that, the better your content will be. What makes content great is when you make it about helping by either saving the reader time or money, or making their life or business easier. It is that simple. And if you can get the reader to laugh or feel inspired in the process, then you have a content home run. Stories, aka content, that move emotion are what make people forward, repost, comment, and ultimately connect.

Create story hooks for media pick up

Whenever you create content for a client or yourself, of course you should make sure you always have some type of story hook in the piece. Take it a step further and only focus on your brand's direct reader. Also focus on multiple media outlet readers. Always ask yourself: Where could this be featured? What type of media—newspaper, magazine, television, or radio—would pick this up because it is exactly what their readers, viewers, or listeners want? That is why a hook is so important. It is what makes your story newsworthy. It is something that will attract editors and producers because it attracts the attention of their readers or viewers.

To do this, first things first. You need to observe the media outlets you choose to watch or read and figure out: What hooks you? What gets your attention? Write some of these things down. Also, ask a few of your top customers what they are interested in hearing about in terms of your industry or the products or services your company offers, and where they find their new product or service information. Check out those outlets as well. This is an excellent question to add into a customer survey.

Some stories come with hooks already in the story. For example, a local school superintendent of 30 years announcing his retirement is a newsworthy story because this event is rare or unique. It does not need an extra hook to generate interest. Here are a few hook ideas to help get you started:

- *Something new or never been seen*. Ground-breaking or first-ever
- *A fresh angle on an old story*. New research shows previous assumption invalid
- *Localization of a national news story*. Emphasize local impact on a national breaking story
- *Anticipated trends*. People want to be up-to-date, so offer three to five facts as to why that new trend is emerging
- *Controversy*. Where there is disagreement there is a story

- *Celebrity*. If a celebrity is involved with a product you carry or visited your location, this is a great way to get the media's attention

Create content using the top tips approach

The time has arrived. You are here. Yep, you are now going to learn all about taking your story hooks and adding them into the creation of your top tips. Top tips are simple to create. They do not take much time, and the media as well as readers consider them to be quality content. They are an excellent way to build your credibility with your audience. Your tips should include an approach of saving your reader time or money and be direct advice from you. This is what will set you apart in the online community. These are great to use for blog posts as well as for the media. Top tips are approximately 750 words in length, and they have a specific format the media prefers. You can also expand your top tips into an article brief of 1,250 to 1,500 words. The media loves these because they are so easy to just pick up and reprint. An article brief elaborates on a top tip or a certain subject.

Have your team and/or customers submit ideas to you. For top tip examples, go to www.StarrHall.com.

To get started, make a list of top four to five tips and/or advice you would offer your target market regarding your offerings. An example might be "Top Five Tips for Social Networking" for a high-level networker (HLN, remember?).

Figure 9.1 contains a questionnaire to take you through the process of creating your own top tips.

To get you started with your mobile messaging, consider the following top tips example for "The Power of Mobile Marketing" as published by *Entrepreneur* magazine online:

1. *Choose a simple keyword that is easy to text*. Most of your customers will join your mobile program by sending a text message to a short code number (5 or 6 digits) with a keyword to identify your program. Your customer may have limited time to read

TOP TIPS QUESTIONNAIRE

1. If you were to write an article for your target market or campaign, what would the title be and why? _____

   _____

2. When writing or compiling your tips, ask yourself this question: Why should I care? When you ask this question, you will find it helps you come up with tips that are different, of interest, and valuable. _____

   _____

3. The best top tips are based on an angle or advice none of your competitors can come close to matching or knowing. What do you know about your industry or market that they don't? _____

   _____

4. Avoid general tips and general titles. For example: Top Five Steps to Create a Business Plan (boring). Way better is: Top Five Ways to Create a Business Plan in 1 Hour or Less! _____

   _____

5. Keep the subject line or the title short and catchy. Ask yourself: "Would I read or open this?" _____

   _____

6. Keep your tips down to one page, with no more than three sentences per tip. The shorter, the better. You can always elaborate for the media and/or your target market and turn it into an article. _____

   _____

figure 9.1–Top tips questionnaire

your marketing material and have to remember both a short dial number and the keyword to text, so keep it short and make sure it's easy to spell!

2. *Decide what relationship you want to develop with your customer.* You are not trying to build a list of customer mobile numbers so you can SPAM them with a message. Consider collecting a customer's name in the join process so you can personalize all future messages you send. Personalizing your text broadcasts can increase your response rates, but be careful not to overstep relationship boundaries too quickly. This must feel genuine to your customer.

3. *Make an irresistible offer to join your campaign.* In a world where we are bombarded with so many different advertising messages every day, we want to know what's in it for us. You need to keep this in mind with your marketing. Put yourself in your customer's shoes, and ask what they would really want from you and your business. Build that into the marketing material your user will read or hear. Focus on your call to action that will have customers rushing to text your keyword. Does it stand out? Is it exciting and a no-brainer to join?

4. *Integrate your mobile program into all your marketing activity.* Include the keyword commands to join your mobile opt-in lists in everything you do. This includes your website, email footer, print advertising, retail storefront, your receipts or invoices, products, and even on your mobile phone voice message. If your budget allows, try different keywords for different advertising mediums so you know which is the most successful.

A great way to get your readers' email addresses is by turning your top tips into a free download either via video or PDF download. To boost your top tips delivery, be sure to add pictures to text copy or videos. There's more to content creation than just text. You can jazz up your tips and enhance your multimedia skills at the same time by creating and posting slideshows or digital video reports related to your tops post.

Some tips on how to create additional compelling content:

- *Look for causes and conflict.* If there is a bit of an edge to your brand, you might want to consider the cause-and-conflict approach to help drive edgy content. Wherever there are people who believe strongly in a cause, there are bound to be others who disagree with them. That creates conflict, and conflict is what makes the news, as well as blogs, interesting. So look for the causes and conflicts where you live, or within your industry. Maybe there is a disagreement on industry standards or a local development project that would be moving or endangering wildlife. Whatever the cause, if you write about conflicts like these on your blog, you'll find plenty of readers.

- *Voice your opinion.* There are thousands of bloggers who do nothing but post their opinions all day, but that doesn't mean opinion blogging is a bad thing. It does mean you need to set your own opinion blogging apart by focusing on quality and/originality. Do plenty of reporting to support your arguments, and try to make your writing transparent, succinct, and fun to read.

- *Interview people in your field.* By sharing the love and interviewing other people in your field, whether via video or a print interview, you improve your position as a leader and connector. Video interviews are more powerful and can easily be done and recorded via Skype by using Skype recording software, or Vod-Burner, which enables you to capture you, as well as the person that you are interviewing, on camera.

- *Release news about your industry.* Compile studies, statistics, and industry-changing information, and release it on your site by using paper.li. This site organizes links shared on your Twitter and Facebook into an easy-to-read newspaper format. You can post out and Tweet your paper.li releases to your social connections, as well. This is a great way to gather and share content from others and release it in a newspaper format, 24/7!

- *Post your presentations.* There are some amazing new presentation tools available online nowadays. Say goodbye to good ol' boring PowerPoint and hello to SlideRocket and Prezi. These sites have demo and trial versions, but you will probably fall in love with both, jump right over and sign up. Your presentations will improve dramatically. Once you get past the learning curve with these programs, you will find they are well worth the time invested. For examples of Prezi or SlideRocket presentations, visit www.socialwavebook.com.

How and where to post your content online

So you have created all of this amazing content. Now what? Well, friends, it is time to make it available to the masses online. You would be doing this world a grave disservice by not sharing your great tips, so let's do this! First let's start with how to post your content online. Remember the goal is to get people from social sites to visit your foundation—your website. In order to do that, you need to start by posting your top tips on your blog or website. Do a short post with the title of your top tips in your status boxes on social sites such as Twitter, Facebook, and LinkedIn so they go on the newsfeed as well as your profile. For the example we just looked at, the status update would look like: The power of mobile marketing (insert tiny url to go back to your blog here).

The next step in posting this out on your social sites is to do what's called "title switching." Take that same top tips post for the next two to four weeks and switch the titles. For example, a couple of days after posting the previous status update, you would post *Is mobile marketing right for your business?* (Insert tiny url to go back to your blog here, i.e., Figure 9.2.) Do you see how this works? The reason why title switching can be so effective is that different titles can pull in people with different interests. In addition, because you are posting this same top tips out for two to four weeks in a row and at different times during the day, you will most likely reach different people, because people are always coming and going online.

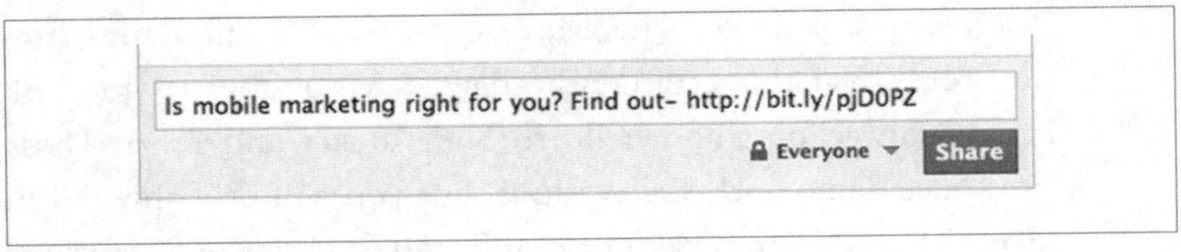

Is mobile marketing right for you? Find out- http://bit.ly/pjD0PZ

🔒 Everyone ▼   Share

figure 9.2–Title switching post

Now you know where to post your titles and links back to your content via status updates and newsfeeds. Take it to another level by posting these same titles with links in discussion groups and forums. LinkedIn is an excellent place to post in its groups section. Now, with that said, make sure your content is in line with the focus of the group. In order to take your post from a link post to an actual discussion (using the top tips example in this book), use wording like: "What do you think about mobile marketing? As the title for the discussion post add-in mentions, I have come up with a few tips on it (insert link back to your site)." Now, the next part is key in making it an even more powerful discussion. You need to end the post with: "What is your experience with mobile marketing"? or "If you have any tips or experiences with mobile marketing you would like to discuss or share, please do so, I would love to get your take on this." It is that wording and close that actually makes it a discussion. Furthermore, you can take this discussion post and send it out to your contacts as well as your media list (which we will get to in Chapter 12).

Podcasting your content

Podcasting is not a new concept or marketing vehicle; it has actually been around for quite some time. Podcasting simply means recording audio and casting it out on the internet. As podcasts increase in popularity, and they do still hold a strong place online, listeners now have more choices. If you are already into podcasting, you might be ahead of the competition but you should still be thinking about ways you can make your podcast unique and stand out from similarly themed podcasts. So let's dig in to this real quick.

When making the decision and commitment to podcast, it is important to think beyond the moment.

- How will podcasting fit into a current marketing schedule, and how frequently will you podcast?
- How will hosting of podcasting files be handled? If the podcast is excessively popular, how will fees be generated to pay for hosting?
- What will make you distinct or different from others podcasting about similar content?

By approaching podcasting with a little forethought, you will set yourself up for success.

Just like any media company, in order to attract and maintain an audience, you need to provide original content, or at the very least, present the content in an original way. Taking your top tips and simply reading them with some enthusiasm incorporated with a bit of humor or short storytelling can really make a podcast stand out. With that said, although jibber jabber is fun, make sure you include quality content. If you have a point to make, make it in a reasonable amount of time. Also make sure you do your homework. Not only is faulty information a liability, incorrect information will hurt a broadcaster's long-term reputation; it is just like being a journalist. Credibility is paramount to success, and it is important that the information you provide be accurate. While being a shock jock might have short-term appeal to listeners, most will remain loyal to a source that has properly researched and relayed all of their information.

Podcasts should contain compelling content with episodic titles that are united in a common broad theme. Each show should be about

> A podcast is an audio file you create in .mp3 format that is uploaded with an RSS (Really Simple Syndication) file to your server. Your target market can download it on any number of programs created to receive or subscribe to your audio file so they can listen to it at their leisure on their computer or a personal mp3 device.

the same length and contain your information in a format that is consistent for your brand and content that is timeless, has a long shelf life, and can be easily archived. How-to content that solves problems (hello, top tips!) will often have long-term appeal and listening life.

The quality of the audio content is extremely important as well. Think of the last time you heard a good song, on a poorly tuned radio station. Regardless of how much you like the song, you will probably change the station.

What you need to podcast: a microphone, audio software, and a hosting account to upload and store your podcast file.

Once you have created your amazing content for your podcast, make sure you really take the time to optimize the title and incorporate data that relates to the contents of the podcast. Think about the themes when selecting a podcast channel title and description. Use critical and related keywords and phrases that relate to a common theme. The text in the feed is important for both feed optimization and for attracting listeners. Many of the podcast directories index the contents of podcasts using the information contained in the channel and item's titles and descriptions. Use these text fields to effectively capture the interest of listeners.

Many new listeners will want to review previous broadcasts, so consider ways to make older shows available through archives. Archives allow broadcasters another channel to benefit from the content. Maintaining archives of older podcasts might bring in new listeners and satisfy listeners who just can't get enough. Podcasts require effort, but by following basic guidelines and thinking things through, podcasts can be instrumental in increasing web traffic and communications within a community.

Steps to creating and launching a podcast journey online

1. *Get a microphone.* To record a podcast, you need to have a microphone that is compatible with your computer.

2. *Get audio software.* You need to get software that allows you to record audio through that microphone and save it on your computer's hard drive. Garageband and/or Audacity are great online recording programs.

3. *Prepare your podcast content.* Take some time to think about what you're going to say during your podcast. Start with your top tips.

4. *Record your podcast.* Turn on your microphone, start your audio software, and begin recording. Save the file when you're done.

5. *Open an account with a podcast host, where you can store your podcasts.* This makes more sense than hosting your podcasts on your website because audio files require quite a lot of storage space, and as your audience grows you will need a lot of bandwidth. Podcast hosting sites are specifically designed to handle those issues for you. Start off with a free, or low-cost account, and think about upgrading when you start to get a good following for your podcast. Popular podcast hosting services include Libsyn, Podbean, HipCast, GoDaddy, OurMedia, and Odeo Studio.

6. *No matter what hosting account you have already chosen or set up, make sure you also upload to iTunes.* After you have recorded a couple of shows and have opened an account with a podcasting host, your next step will be to post your show on iTunes, which is incredibly easy to do. You need to have iTunes, a free download at the iTunes store, installed on your computer. Open iTunes, and click on "iTunes Store." When the store opens, you will see a bar at the top of the browser with "Podcasts" in the middle of the bar. Click on "Podcasts," and on the new page you will see a "Podcasts— podcasts Quick Links" menu column on the right hand side. Click on "Submit a Podcast," and you'll be taken to a new page with a field called "Podcast Feed URL." The podcast feed

Some great podcasting sites to upload and list on: Podcastalley.com, podcastpickle.com, www.digitalpodcast.com, www.podcastbunker.com, www.podcast.com, www.podcastdirectory.com, and iTunes.

will be in the administrative area of your podcasting host site. If you use Podbean, you will find it under "My Profile." Simply copy the feed, paste it into the iTunes "Podcast Feed URL" field, and click "Continue" to go through the submission process. iTunes will soon start showing your podcast, and you can now consider yourself to be in podcasting business!

7. *Create a new blog post, give it a title, and add any text you'd like to introduce your podcast.* Paste the URL for your podcast file into your new blog post as new media or a new link, depending on the blogging application you use. Make sure you open your new live blog post and select your podcast link to ensure it's working correctly.

WIPEOUT

I do not know how to write quality content nor do I have the time. Should I outsource or use a subscription service to provide content that is specific to my industry?

WAVE TIP

You can go to Odesk.com or guru.com and post that you are looking for a writer to provide marketing and blog content. Post your budget, set up a time to Skype interview for an hour, and make it happen. You name the budget and you choose the expert. After you give them a good feel for what your company is about, you can also do a "voice and tone check" by asking them to provide a quick blog post for your company to see how they write about your brand. Make sure they have the same voice and tone that you would use to write and/ or portray your brand.

Dealing with spam online

Spam is so dang annoying, and the more you put yourself out there, the more likely you are to receive spam and it can be time consuming online. Unfortunately, spam isn't going away anytime soon, but there are a few things that you can do to receive less of it and not get caught up in what are called spam links. From junk emails and fake bank transfer advertisements, to bogus comments on websites, spam is a very real (and irritating) part of online life.

As social site platforms continue to emerge and grow, the spam problem, both from other users and from applications, becomes a more pressing concern. Facebook is doing a lot to help reduce what is called app-generated spam, reporting that their platform spam was down 95 percent in 2010, but no automated system is perfect, especially when the platform is as large as Facebook. Wall attacks frequently lead users to agree to install a Facebook application that requires that a user authorize the ability to post to walls and friend pages. Sometimes the scams are easy to detect, with wording like, "OMG you have to check this out," or "You can't miss this!" or something else that is so tempting that you just have to find out what it is. Oh yeah, spammers are sneaky and some of them very clever. Sometimes however, the scams can replicate promotions or apps that really do exist.

Here are some tips to reduce the amount of spam that you see on Facebook, and avoid contributing to the problem yourself.

- Beware of short links that accompany text on your wall from people who don't normally post links.
- Pay attention to what apps you authorize to post to your wall.
- Investigate or research any app that seems too good to be true before agreeing to install it.
- Visit your Facebook privacy settings and click on the bottom section that says "Apps and Websites" to customize your settings. You will see a listing of the most recently accessed apps from

your account. Select the offending app and remove it from your account.

- Delete any messages posted by the app on your behalf and notify any friends that might have been spammed.
- Also keep an eye out for popular scams and waves of attacks.

Another type of spamming that happens on Twitter is called "follow spam." It is the act of following mass numbers of people, not because the person is actually interested in their tweets, but simply to gain attention, get views of your profile (and possibly clicks on URLs therein), or (ideally) to get followed back. Many people who are seeking to get attention in this way have even created programs to do the following on their behalf, which enable them to follow thousands of people at the blink of any eye.

In extreme cases, these automated accounts can follow so many people, Twitter posted on their blog, that "they actually threaten the performance of the entire Twitter system." In less-extreme cases, they simply annoy thousands of legitimate users who get an email about this new follower only to find out their interest may not be entirely sincere. Additionally, there are Tweeters and what are called "bots" (short for "robots") out there that start accounts just to follow key words and then send out Tweets that spam people who are using those keywords. A few quick things that you can do to get less of this is to mask or obscure the names of any brands or types of businesses in your tweets. Spammers set up these bots to automatically follow and spam any mention of their target industry. For example, a spammer with a mobile phone marketing scheme might program a Twitter spam account to automatically follow anyone who mentions mobile, text message, or iPhone. A spammer with an eBay affiliate link will automatically follow anyone who mentions eBay. For this reason, it's best to obscure or mask the mention of any brand name or type of business. Leave a space between letters ("mo bile" instead of "mobile") or use an asterisk to mask the name of the product or business ("N*tflix" instead of "Netflix"). This will throw auto-follow spam bots off the scent of your Tweets.

You can Tweet that you just arrived in Las Vegas, and within 30 seconds receive a half-dozen Tweets that spam you with iPhone specials, and even a car special. A few Las Vegas shows and Tweets on Las Vegas clubs will come through as well—legitimate businesses following their keywords and sending you information and offers to get you to their business during your stay—that's smart spamming. Hey, you never know, maybe you'll need specially discounted tickets to go see the Le Rêve show and just didn't know it yet.

10

GET OFF OF THE ISLAND

improve your social skills online

> *If you don't have daily objectives, you qualify as a dreamer.*
> —Zig Ziglar

How you post and respond is key in building your contacts, connections, and relationships. Words can hardly express how important it is to have a response system for your social networking efforts. You can save yourself and your clients thousands of hours of grief by following proper response etiquette, also known as "netiquette," using the 3/3 rule. Here are a few things to help improve time management online as well as build respectful relationships.

Response etiquette

- There is no need to respond to posts, emails, and replies that thank you for posting or sharing something. Basically, you do not need to thank someone for thanking you.

- Only respond to people who ask you a question, are requesting more information, or require a response for brand control reasons, meaning if someone posts something rude or mouthy in regard to one of your posts, or if something they said in a comment or post needs to be explained or corrected, you simply reply shortly and sweetly (and no, that doesn't mean dripping with sarcasm).
- Set one to two times per week to respond to all inquiries and notifications unless they are time sensitive. You need to determine what time sensitive is for your business and industry. You may decide all non-urgent emails get answered twice a week and urgent emails get attention once a day. Unless a house is on fire, or someone you love is in need, everything else can wait while you deal with your time-sensitive email.

Become HIP

Step outside of your comfort zone every once in awhile. Five times per day would be a great start. Take that stepping-out time to post some really cool stuff and be HIP online:

- *Humor.* Get funny, play a bit, post humorous videos, cartoons, jokes that have to do with your industry. You can even poke fun at yourself. YouTube is here to save the day, as an excellent resource for funny stuff. StumbleUpon has always had great comical sites and posts that they send out as well. People are always looking online for funny stuff to break up their day. Without laughter, what else is there really? People love to laugh, and studies have shown that it actually can help someone connect faster in a new relationship. Eighty-seven percent of users on Match.com had reported that they connected quicker when someone's profile had a sense of humor or jokes in it.
- *Inspire.* Add some motivation to people's days; we all need it. Even a motivational speaker needs motivation! Whether this is an inspiring quote, short story, or even encouraging news and

statistics about your industry, sharing inspiration can change a person's energy, brighten their day, and even prompt them to reach out to you. Be a day brightener!

- *Pull.* Get people to interact with you more by pulling them into conversation. One of the best ways to do this is to get curious and ask questions. "What do you think about this?" Or, "I came across this site today and I like this; what do you think?" "Have you ever. . .", and so on. Questions cause people to take action and become involved, especially when it is a topic that they are particularly interested in. You might find some questions posted on your social sites can generate 150 comments in just minutes. When this happens, don't just let these comments run—get involved in between and respond so they feel heard. If you don't, then chances are next time you post a question, they will not be as motivated to contribute.

Asking for the business using the 3/3 rule

As you are meeting new people online, having conversations, posting away, building exposure and handling new opportunities daily, you are going to have to draw the line at some point with the back and forth, also known as time wasters. If someone is continually asking for your advice, free product, tips, and so forth, when responding, do it no more than 3 times, spending a maximum of 3 minutes each time, before you ask for the business. If the contact does not respond or decides to not do business with you, there is no need to offer additional expert advice and/or tips and guidance for free. People will respect you if you respect yourself and the value of your experience and advice by adhering to the 3/3 boundary formula. If you spend even a few hours every week going back and forth with the same person who is never going to do business with you, then you might need to keep your day job.

If your business revenue has either leveled off or declined, it's worth looking into whether your sales team is asking or has stopped asking

---

A SAMPLE OF A 3/3 RESPONSE

Hello, Mrs. Smith!

Thank you again for reaching out to me, I was glad to hear that you received guidance from my tips and suggestions for your project.

To date, I have offered you 2 consults via email, as well as a quick call. I would like to continue working with you to help grow your business in the following areas by [insert examples here].

If you would like to move forward with my services, I have attached my rate sheet for your review and immediate consideration. If you are not yet ready to commit to a working relationship, please do keep in touch and let me know when you are ready to proceed.

I look forward to hearing from you.

To our continued success,

[Close with your name and/or company here]

---

figure 10.1–A sample of a 3/3 response

for the business. If you find they are doing constant back and forth, finger-crossing in the hope they will eventually get the buy from a customer, adapt the example in Figure 10.1 to help cut to the chase and send an email, note, or even make a phone call to ask for the business. This example will do wonders for your business. As always with scripts, make this one your own; add in your brand personality.

Definition of asking

When it comes to asking, "Ask and you shall receive; don't, and you shall be late on your rent (or mortgage)!" Look at the word "ask" as standing for: Always Seek Knowledge, and add to that, business!

So why don't most people ask for what they want? First of all, most people don't even know what it is they want, which causes a delay in asking before you even start. What exactly do you want from the people you talk to and communicate with, whether it is online or in person? You need to determine what this is. Start by writing out the top three things that you would like from the people that you meet. Maybe it is connections, maybe you want to make a certain dollar amount per contact, or you may want to access their knowledge. Get in the habit of asking people who you meet the very first time, "What would you like from me, how can I help? Ninety-nine percent of the time you'll find people looking back at you like a deer in headlights. Be patient while people figure out how to respond.

The second reason people don't ask for what they want is the fear of rejection, or on the other end of that, the fear of success. Just do it! If the person says no, it's no loss because you weren't doing anything with them prior to you asking. There is always someone else at the next turn ready and willing to cooperate with you.

Figure 10.2 on page 144 contains a few quick scripts that you can build from to get you asking for what you want online.

Levying the power of ASK

To impress upon you the importance and power of asking, here are a few examples of successful asking:

- By asking for emails on your blog posts, you can greatly increase your email database by broadcasting the posts through Twitter and LinkedIn.
- Get booked for paid speaking engagements by looking for opportunities in conversations around your area of expertise and asking to be the speaker.
- Secure a book publishing deal by looking for publishing professionals in your industry on LinkedIn and asking if they would publish your book and telling them why they should in just two paragraphs!

ONLINE OR EMAIL MESSAGE AFTER MAKING A NEW CONNECTION

Thank you for the connection, I look forward to getting to know you.

So, let's get started. What can we do to help each other grow our business or person connections? List share, send a few tips back and forth, contribute to each other's blogs, connect one another with a few influential people or industry leaders that we know?

Let me know your thoughts; let's find a creative way to make this happen.

Kindly,

[Your name, credentials, and website]

ON THE PHONE

Hello __(contact name)_____, my name is _____. We haven't met yet, and I know that you are busy, so I will be brief. I was impressed with your [profile/website/event—whichever is appropriate] and I would like to ask for 15 minutes of your time to determine if there is a way that we can help each other grow our personal or professional network and/or business. Would you be open to that?

IN PERSON

Adapt the telephone script above. However, if you have no idea what your new contact does for a living, or if they are a connector or someone that you would like to meet, add this in:

> Do you have a goal to grow your personal or professional network? I think there may be way that we can help each other. Let's set aside 15 minutes either right now or in the near future via phone to determine needs and how our networks can help each other. Are you open to that?

---

figure 10.2–Scripts to adapt for asking contacts for what you want

- Invite your contacts to sign up for a free monthly teleconference. You might start with only 25 on a call, but if you stay with it, you can have several thousand people on your telecalls before you know it.
- You could secure monthly paid columns on major media and blogs sites such as American Express Small Business Open and an exposure column on *Entrepreneur* magazine online.
- Secure new clients weekly by simply letting them know how you can help them (give specific details, not generalizations), and then just ask! Become an asking machine.

QUICK ASKING TIPS

A very powerful asking technique when you are calling someone or starting a conversation is to engage their need to be helpful: "Hi, yes, I am hoping that you can help me," or "Hi there, how can I help you with a project that you are currently working on?" or "There is someone I know that may be able to help you with what you are working on, let me introduce you," or "There is a great video or book I believe that can help you with that (name whatever it is they are working on, or their business industry)." Use these trust lines day in and day out. They will help you build your connections and business worldwide and to levels that simply aren't possible without asking.

Offer teleseminars

Teleseminars are still a favorite way to reach out and connect with your market. If done right, teleseminars can be very powerful and effective for most any brand, product or service, business to consumer, business to business, or person to person relationship. Let's explore this possibility for you and add some extra super cool ways to really power up teleseminars for your brand.

It really doesn't take much to host your own teleseminar. All you need is a few tools, many of which are either free or very affordable. To host your own teleseminars you of course need a phone and what is called a bridge line, or conference center. This bridge line will allow the callers to hear all others, similar to three-way calling, but with bigger numbers. In this conferencing service, you, as the moderator, can control a call. You can mute the call so you are the only one who can speak, or you can let everyone speak. Be sure that you find a bridge line that allows recording because you should be recording every single teleseminar that you do so you can not only send it to people that couldn't make the live call, but also to assess yourself and see where you can improve. You can also provide a transcript of your recording as a resource on your site, or as a giveaway. You can get thousands of people to your teleseminar with FreeConferenceCalling.com, which offers quality service and great recordings, all for the incredible price of zero. If you are planning on doing many of them, check out a paid service like Welcome to the Call (http://WelcomeToTheCall.com/ProductInfo/?x=2618596). It comes with more bells and whistles and allows people to listen at their computer, or dial in with Skype. Every time you schedule a live teleseminar, jump on the line with a friend or one of your VAs (virtual assistants) to make sure the line is working properly and that you know how to access the functions available, such as record, unmute all lines, or mute all lines, etc.

Teleseminar calls may last for 30 minutes up to a few hours, based on the kind of teleseminar. Anything over an hour is often too much for people to sit through, and it is a lot to ask, whether they are paying you or not.

Avoid sending your prospects to "landing page hell" when you want them to sign up or register for your teleseminar. There is no need for this type of approach any longer as it turns people off, and it is not great for branding. You do, however, need some type of registration link or opt-in page. This page or link should be clean, light, and to the point. You can use sites such as EventBrite or Lanyrd, but sometimes a one-page micro website or adding a page for the event to your WordPress site works just as well. You can also use a free service such as Weebly.

Once you get people to register through an email capture (we will cover exactly how those work in Chapter 13), it is very important that you set up an auto-response email so you can automatically email the confirmation and call-in details. You also need to set up automatic reminder emails, so your audience doesn't forget to call in.

So, how do you get people to this registration page to sign up? Here are the top five ways that you can promote your teleseminar.

1. *Facebook and LinkedIn events.* Post your event on Facebook and send it out to your friends. Because it isn't location specific, you can send it to most anyone you are connected to on Facebook. Remember to keep the invite brief and mention that if they aren't interested, perhaps they could pass it on to someone who is.

2. *Teaser posts.* Start posting a few weeks prior to your event on Twitter, Facebook, and LinkedIn, using teasers that will give a hint to a tip or a resource that you will be sharing on the call. Adding a few humor posts are a great way to grab people's attention as well.

3. *Send a notice to your email list.* Do not forget your friends, family, vendors, networking lists, and of course, your email database. Even if your list is 20 people, send away.

4. *Use keyword search functions.* Jump on Twitter, LinkedIn, and Facebook to find conversations or posts by keyword. Once you find people having conversations about your topic, send them a message, Tweet them, invite them in.

5. *Do a giveaway.* In order to entice people even more to register and show up, offer them a free download, a free book, virtual gift card, or something that has value. You can also partner with another website or company. For example, if you specialize in golf country club real estate sales, partner with an online company to offer 100 free memberships to golf clubs around the globe.

Making the most of your teleseminar

An advantage of teleseminars is that many of your prospective clients who are interested in your services will be able to ask you questions regarding certain issues they have during a question-and-answer period. Teleseminars are a great tool to earn money via your expertise as well. This is a win-win situation, because the reduced overhead means less cost for your client as well as the convenience of staying in their homes, and the lowered costs mean you will earn more through teleseminars! Get a few under your belt before you start charging away. If you break it down, you can actually earn more cash per hour than when you're giving one-on-one conferencing. For example, you will charge $300 an hour for the one-on-one conference services. If you are charging $50 per person, per hour on teleseminar, and 10 people avail of it, you'll be earning $500 an hour; this is larger than the physical seminar but with a similar length of time!

Designing your teleseminar

When putting a teleseminar together, here are a few things you need to know:

1. *Do not choose a saturated topic.* Try to avoid a topic that everyone in your market is hammering at your prospects as well. This can be a tricky sin to avoid and here's why: You need to find the right balance between issues that are top of mind and ones that are overdone. For example, the current economy is certainly a top-of-mind issue, but at some point, teleseminars about doing X, Y, and Z in a down economy are going to fall on deaf ears. So if you do this topic, you have to do it with a twist, and add some power to it.

2. *Avoid a generic title.* The title of your teleseminar is a make-or-break success factor. In fact, many of your prospects will decide whether or not to register for your call based solely on what it's called. Example: Let's say you're doing a teleseminar for deal-

ing with divorce. A generic title would be, *How to Move on After Divorce*. Not bad; this title makes a promise. It's better than simply, *Divorce 101*. But a better title hits an emotional appeal. An example of this is, *Move Past Your Divorce in 30 Days or Less: How to Deal with Your Anger and Emotions and Feel Great in Less than 30 Days*. See the difference?

3. *Do not forget about collecting intelligence information when getting registrations.* Imagine how many callers you'd be able to close if you only knew exactly what your prospects wanted and exactly how to sell it to them. Well, finding out is simpler than you ever thought possible. Ask. On your registration form, include a section for your registrants to fill in their biggest question relating to your teleseminar. You'll be shocked how open and honest their questions are, and how easy they make planning, delivering, and closing your teleseminar. Once you know what they want, you can tailor your call so it speaks directly to their pain or desires.

4. *Don't forget the follow through.* Just because they signed up doesn't mean they'll show up. In fact, if you neglect to remind your registrants about your call, less than 25 percent of them will be there. People are busy, and they're likely to forget the exact date and time of your call if you don't remind them several times. So, send a minimum of three reminders. And use the reminders as a way to re-excite them about your teleseminar by including enticing, bulleted points that tease the content of the call. That way they'll remember both when to be there and why they should.

5. *Include handout.* A lot of people ignore handouts because they seem like a lot of extra work; they aren't. When you use your handouts the right way, you do two things: You satisfy your registrants' need for instant gratification and you increase your show-up rate. When you give your prospects a "sneak peek" of your content, you heighten their desire and curiosity even

more. Just be sure not to reveal too much. You don't want your registrants to look at your handouts, assume they know everything there is to know, and not show up for your call.

6. *Stop waiting for perfection.* There is no such thing as a perfect teleseminar or webinar—let's just clear that up right now or you will waste months, even years, trying to achieve one. It's more important to get a teleseminar done quickly rather than perfectly (especially your first teleseminar). Even when things don't go as planned, if you're offering something your callers desperately want, you're going to make money. Don't wait. Each call will get better and more profitable as you tweak and revise the last.

Some ideas for your teleseminar are:

• Updates and news about your industry

WIPEOUT

I am not a very social person offline, let alone online. What other things can I do other than post and engage with people?

WAVE TIP

You can hire someone to be social for you. If that isn't in your budget, then utilize other people's postings, videos, and content that are related to your industry, yet not competition, and post it on your social sites as well as blog or website. For example, a fitness trainer might post content and videos that have to do with nutrition or vitamins; this compliments what the fitness trainer offers, yet is not competition. Make sure you get permission if it is someone else's content.

- How-to
- Giveaways and Contests
- Interviews
- Announcements
- Top Tips

Truthfully, the only difference between you and a profitable teleseminar expert is time.

11

HOW TO CONVERT SMALL FISH INTO BIG FISH

turning relationships into sales

> *What you do speaks so loudly that I cannot hear what you say.*
> —RALPH WALDO EMERSON

The thinking around doing business has undergone a sea change since the internet became easily accessible worldwide. Instead of having an attitude that people are out to get you in the business world, the internet is making people think: People are out to do business with you; why not be generous with them? Generosity is one of the main reasons that people buy from brands. When people willingly share their knowledge and expertise online, the business always seems to follow. The more generous you are with your expertise and resources, the faster people will connect with you online and want to do business with you. Don't be impatient and act desperate; people can smell the difference between desperate and sincere. Make sure that you really want the relationship and their business, specifically, and that you're not just asking for the sake of getting another deal, or because it's your third action and you're

153

"supposed" to get the deal. Consumers are smart and they can tell the difference between the two.

Check the SPAM at the door

It is wise to exercise caution when building sincere relationships and not have sales-pitch conversations with people you know. Before you even ask for the business, when you're beginning to build a relationship, you need to do a SPAM check. That is, whether it be online or off, make sure that your conversation does not involve constant Sales Pitching After Meeting. If you start a sales pitch before you've even established a rapport, then you are spamming, something that consumers do not tolerate very well, and can instantly shut down a relationship. Make the conversation about the consumer, not you. Start by listening, and end conversations by asking what you can do to help them with a goal or problem. By doing this, your services and offerings will become a natural part of the conversation, rather than a forced sales pitch. Remember to be yourself and do not, repeat, do not, try to be someone that you are not in order to get more contacts, leads, and business. Consumers want to feel like they are doing business with someone real, not someone who's insincere.

Above all, don't hold yourself back from reaching out to new people, groups, or industries. The internet is full of millions of new contacts for you; just engage with them sincerely and leave out the sales pitching. You never know if that invite or accepted request will be your next big customer.

Building your social proof

Social proof is not a new concept by any means, it simply has a new approach. In the most basic terms, it means that you prove that you are worth doing business with, and that you are the one to go to, not your competitor. If someone is looking to hire a speaker and they check your LinkedIn profile as well as Suzy Speaker, if they see that your profile has over 130 recommendations on it, with a link to over 200 more, and they look at Suzy's profile and they see that she only has two, who are they most likely to hire? It is a no-brainer. With all of the review and recommendation sites online, you have an amazing opportunity to build your proof portfolio.

Do you have testimonials or recommendations on your social sites and your main website or blog? Testimonials show potential clients and customers how great you are, you don't have to say a thing. LinkedIn is a great place to house some of those testimonials. See Figure 11.1 on page 156 for a script to help you reach out to your LinkedIn connections to start networking recommendations.

Also consider getting video testimonials from people who attend your events or even a client meeting. Take your flip cam with you wherever you go (it's small enough to fit in a purse!) and be ready to flip it open and record. You can ask simple questions such as, "Can you tell me about (their experience with you, services you provided, or your product)?" If your clients are miles or continents away, simply ask them to web cam their endorsement and send the file your way. If they are happy with you, they will gladly do this, and the worst they can say is "no." You will never know until you ask! One of the fastest and easiest ways to send larger video files is Yousendit.com, which offers a free version that allows you to send up to 100MB; anything over that is only $10 a month, for this oh-so-worthy service.

Using your warm list

People who you already know and with whom you have built a mutually trustworthy relationship—warm people—are the fastest, easiest way to get referrals and new business. It is time that you reach out to them online. You would be surprised at how many people you know are active online. Start by reaching out and reconnecting with the top 25 people in your center of influence that respect or admire you. This could be friends from grammar or high school, college alumni, past coworkers,

---

SOCIAL PROOF SCRIPT

Send this script directly from your LinkedIn account to connections online. If you don't have a LinkedIn account yet or you only have two connections, get busy and commit.

Hello to my fabulous and wonderful LinkedIn connection. I had a thought today, and wanted to run it by you. With a goal of building my social proof (aka recommendations and reviews) to over 100 within the next 30 days, I thought,- why don't we check each other out (websites, services, etc.), and provide a recommendation [note: if you have already worked together] or a review of products or services by taking time to check each other out?

Maybe you have [insert your product or services here, e.g.: read my column in *Entrepreneur* magazine or at American Express Small Business Open, have heard me speak, read my book etc.]. I would love and appreciate a review/ recommendation and, of course, in return I will take the time to check you out online and provide the same. Isn't this what networking is all about, getting to know each other on a deeper level? I look forward to possibly working with you and trying out your product and/or service.

If you are not able or willing to provide, no worries; just ignore my request.

Here is to our continued success,

[insert your name, credentials, and website address here]

figure 11.1–Social proof script

family members, best-selling authors, media contacts, etc. Make sure the 25 that you choose are active users online. If you cannot locate 25 active warm users on social sites, then email these contacts directly. Your goal in reconnecting with these 25 people is to reach out to them, send an email brief and ask what they are up to in their life and/or business. I have even created a quick script for you to make your own and send away.

EMAIL OR POSTING SAMPLE

Hello [contact's name],

It's been a while since I have checked in with you. How [is/are] the [family, children, dog, etc.; this must be something personal]?

I noticed that you are now [insert something about job or career here]. Are you enjoying it? How long have you been [insert career, industry or job title here]?

[OPTIONAL]Do you remember when we used to [insert a memory from childhood, work, family; something that applies to this contact], that was so [insert adjective: wonderful, funny, hilarious, etc.]

Just wanted to drop you a note to say hello, would love to catch up. Feel free to email back at your convenience.

I look forward to hearing from you.

Kindly,

[insert name here]

figure 11.2–Email or posting sample

Creating friend lists on social sites

Being able to organize your connections by lists on social sites is one of the coolest capabilities available. You can now separate out and keep track of your connections by client, prospect, friends, family, and what's called GTK (getting to know). They are also a great way to target privacy settings on sites like Facebook.

On Facebook, you can also filter your view of each list's stream of activity separately in the news feed on your homepage. This way, you can view all of your client's posts on the news stream at a time or check in with just your friends. You can also set what pictures or posts you want certain friends or lists to see or not see. It is really easy to create these lists on Facebook by clicking the "Account" drop-down menu at the top of any page, and then click on "Edit Friends." Click the "Create New List" button at the top of the page to create a new list, or type the name of a friend in the left-side search field to add a friend to an existing list. You can also click on an existing friend lists on the left side of the page, and then click on the Edit List button. If you have more than two friend lists, you can easily add or remove friends from lists by using the drop-down menu that appears next to their names on the "All Friends" tab of the Friends page.

Facebook is not the only site that offers list creation. You can do the same thing on LinkedIn with an upgraded account. To upgrade on LinkedIn means to pay for additional capabilities on their site.

Twitter has a little bit different approach to creating and managing lists. When you click to view a list on Twitter, you'll see a stream of Tweets from all the users included in that group or list. You don't need to follow another user to add them to a list, so this is an excellent way to check out people on Twitter without officially "following" them. If you want to read a user's Tweets, but not see their messages in your main timeline every day, lists allow you to do that. Similarly, following someone else's list does not mean you follow all users in that list. Rather, you follow the list itself.

To create a list on Twitter you just visit the profile of the first user you would like to add to your list then click the list drop-down, at the bottom of the drop-down menu, click "Create list," enter the credentials of your list, and choose whether others can see it or whether it is private. Some quick FYIs about Twitter lists: there is a limit of 20 lists per user. List names cannot begin with a numerical character and they cannot exceed 25 characters. There is currently a maximum of 500 accounts allowed on each list, which of course could change. For now, just know that all lists can save you a ton of time online. So go to it, make it happen, set up your lists. Tweet me (@starrhall) when you are done setting up your lists. I want to hear all about your action taking.

Mobile marketing to big fish

One of the best ways to reach out to little fish and make them bigger is to nurture and grow your relationship with them by getting them into a mobile marketing journey (you forgot all about that nasty word "campaign," didn't you?). When your prospects are waiting for a train, or standing in line somewhere, they will pull out their smartphone as a source of engagement and entertainment. Mobile phones connect us to our worlds with a reach well beyond land-line phones, and even the internet. Consumers are connected via voice, SMS, the mobile web, and applications. The mobile phone is being used to manage our lives with banking, GPS, scheduling, games, and even fantasy sports management functionality is now available. Customizing a handset with icon-based links to mobile sites, interesting applications, videos, and of course, unique ringtones has gone mainstream. Make your mobile strategy easy to access and more importantly, relevant and personal. One of my favorite mobile marketing companies is enowit.com. They offer a free trial, great rates, and very personable customer service.

> Keep your text to a minimum, and only send one or two to your list per month, otherwise you might find your opt-out rate is extremely high. Keep in mind that people carry their mobile phones almost everywhere they go to stay connected with friends and family, and you do not want to overwhelm that space.

Ask your customers or clients to "catch it on film"

Increasingly, consumers are using their phones to capture real-time events happening in everyday life. This is a great opportunity for building a relationship and engaging your customers to participate by submitting their own captured moments directly from their mobile devices. Make sure that you cover all aspects of what could go wrong prior to launching. If there are any questions, you really want to know the answers if any of the videos go viral—would the message create a perfect storm or smooth sailing for your company?

Integrate with other marketing mediums

Mobile works best when tied with other media like TV, print, radio, and live events. For example, make sure you have specific mobile landing pages for each of your mobile banners, just like you would on the web.

Give in order to receive

Offer an incentive such as access to relevant information (updated industry information, product releases, events, VIP access, etc.), mobile content, or even a coupon to increase take rates and consumer participation.

If you really want to jump into mobile messaging and create your own mobile apps (applications), then make sure from the start that your goal is to put the user in control. Design your application so when the end user clicks on it, they can control the interaction and choose what to do as they move through your app. If you have any functions such as emailing friends on the app or "check this out" approaches, make sure that you allow that without sending them off of your app.

Mobile messaging lingo

SMS—Short Message Service [max 160 characters]

Keyword—This is the word people would text to opt in on your mobile campaign. You can also add people manually, or use a website widget to automate the opt-in.

Short Code Number—This is the code you provide for your campaign. Example:

> Text "Starr" to 55599. The short code number is 55599.

Once the subscriber texts your keyword to this number, they are subscribed and an auto-message would go out to them, such as

> Thank you for subscribing. To opt out at any time just reply with stop.

---

11 / how to convert small fish into big fish

Also, adding a "skip" button is mandatory, because if users don't see something fun and engaging in a few seconds, you will lose them. Once they are in, create an approach where they can discover information or take them through a quick but engaging story or cartoon.

When building an app, also make sure that the time between clicking the banner and the first user interaction is less than four seconds, and provide a strong CTA (call to action). One of the best ways to ensure that users engage with your ad is to offer them something valuable in return, such as discounts and coupons, free tickets to something online or in their local area, or even free music or other apps. You can even use images for discounts and coupons that automatically save in the photo gallery for easy access later. Sites like Mutualmobile. com or grapplemobile.com can design and create apps for your brand or marketing journey.

Subscription sites

There are some great applications out there where you can build your very own social networking sites for politics, associations, a cause, education, recruitment, and even entertainment. You can also monetize by asking members for a fee, with member billing, and you can charge for premium service with member levels, or just go for the basic site advertising model of Google AdSense and host advertisements. However, if you are building your brand and reputation, leave the mass Google advertising out of the mix on this one. You have no real control over what ads will pop up on your social site, and it just might end up being a company that could either be a competitor (it does happen!) or something that your core values do not support or are in line with. So be careful with this one. A few suggested sites to build this platform are www.ning.com (*ning* means "peace" in Chinese), www.socialgo. com, and now customerhub.com. With CustomerHub, you need to be an InfusionSoft user, but it is worth it. CustomerHub integrates automatically with Infusionsoft to help systemitize your site and your marketing. Ning offers a 30-day trial, however once that is over it is a paid-for service. Socialgo offers both free and premium versions. CustomerHub is a paid-for service.

So what can you do with sites like these? You can launch a subscription-based program or a member-level program. This type of site is not only an excellent revenue model for your business to have automated income, it also serves your focus market at the level they want to do business with you.

At StarrHall.com, the Bronze Starr membership, which is a "freemium" level, allows you access to Starr Hall forums and free marketing resources. The Silver Starr level includes the Bronze plus access to all of Starr Hall's marketing resources and one live call with Starr every month, for a low monthly fee of around $50. At the Gold Starr level, you can access Starr Hall live twice per month, and you get all the benefits of the previous levels plus all of my templates, scripts, and access to its sales and marketing center for $197 per month. Two higher levels, Platinum and Diamond, are for executive-level clients, running at an annual fee of $6,000 and $30,000, respectively. This level structure provides a point of entry and relationship building for every focus market member at the level they are at, both in regard to budget as well as mindset and action taking. The site has automated billing, amazingly easy management tools to easily upload new content, videos, images, etc. This is the next wave and you should not only ride it; you should create some of your own! Check out membership-based sites and consider them for your service line of offerings.

You could also make a membership site work for a product as well. For example, let's say you have a champagne bar. You could launch a VIP Champagne membership club that allows access at different levels to events, champagne pairing tips, videos, etc., with higher-level members receiving monthly champagne and dessert baskets, while at the basic paid-for level members would receive one yummy featured dessert per month. The possibilities with these sites now really are endless.

Nine power steps to turn social into profit

The social profit chart

The days when businesses looked at social network sites as time wasters are quickly fading as people find savvy ways to use socializing to increase revenue and profits. Figure 11.3 on page 164 shows the interconnected flow of everything internet-social. The power steps to supercharging your social profit are as follows:

- *Power-up Profile Info.* Make sure that every social profile you have is completely powered up with rich keywords for your industry and company, and that every single section and box is filled out completely.
- *Connect with Friends/Family.* Do not forget to reach out to the people who already know you, because this can often be your best source of referrals and business.
- *Find Target Market.* Use the advanced search functions given in this book to locate and reach out to your target market online (at search.twitter.com, and/or in Facebook's search box, and/or LinkedIn's advanced search option in the search box)
- *Post Daily.* It is important that you post online, and you can mix this up with bizper posts, personality posts, or just share a funny video, great resource, or even a question. The more you post, the better chance you have of staying active in the news feed, and posting can always help with search engine optimization.
- *Engage More.* It is not just about posting online; you need to take time, every day, whether it is 15 minutes or two hours and talk with people online. Be social! This is what starts to turn relationships into referrals and revenue. It is the same thing in face-to-face encounters; you need to talk and build the relationship to get the sale.
- *Give Valuable Top Tips.* People are always looking for new things and better ways to do them. If you can offer tips and resources on how to make their lives or business easier, save them time and

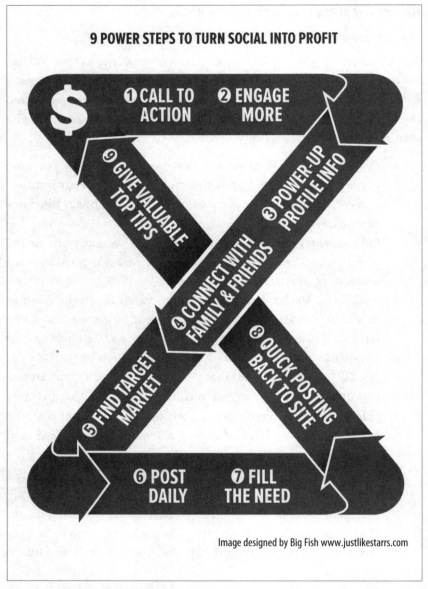

figure 11.3–The social profit chart

11 / how to convert small fish into big fish

money, you are in! Be consistent and post new tips at least once per month.

- *Online Posting Back to Site.* Take your tips from the last step and post them to your social networks with a link back to your site or blog where the tips are hosted. This gets them back to your site, reading about your awesomeness and possibly navigating further. Cha-ching!

- *Call to Action.* You need to make sure that your website visitors are asked to do something once they arrive at your site. If you can only get them to do one thing, what would it be? Give you their email address and name? Or view a video? Whatever it is, try to have no more than two calls to action, and always ask them

WIPEOUT

Do I really need to be on every top social site online?

WAVE TIP

Yes and no. If your target market is not on a particular site, then leave it out., The three major ones—Twitter, Facebook, and LinkedIn—are asking for your presence, along with your customers, and prospects. If you do not have a presence on these sites and your market is trying to find you, talk to you, or see if you are listening, then you are not only missing opportunity but you are telling your market that you are not listening to them online. That's not a good message to send. Don't get overwhelmed with all of the tools, tips, and tricks at once. Just ease into them, find out what works for you and what doesn't in regard to reaching out, connecting, and making moola online.

for their contact information. If you have made the call compelling enough, and they want what you're offering, they will gladly give you their contact information.

- *Fill the Need.* You can always find out what your target market's needs are by simply asking. However, you can also read conversations on your industry sites or in the news feeds by looking up conversations by keywords to determine how you can fill a need, and, hello!, charge for it.

THE TIDAL WAVE APPROACH

social networking for powerful publicity

> If a picture is
> worth a thousand
> words, then an
> article must be worth
> a thousand ads.
> —UNKNOWN

Public relations tools are the most powerful in building your brand. Business startups often need to build their credibility quickly to compete with established competition. By taking advantage of public relations opportunities you can position yourself as an expert in your field, attract media attention, and serve as a quoted source in published articles. As you give interviews and get quoted, professional associations may ask you to give speeches or participate in panel discussions, thus solidifying your credibility.

Why PR works

Emerging-growth entrepreneurs will tell you that it's not enough to win a new customer. You need to convince a newcomer to come back and buy more. By aligning your PR campaign with your goal of attracting repeat business, you can build consumer confidence and trust. For example: By prequalifying some of your best customers on your website, you send a message that you value your clients and share a stake in their success. Also by targeting a group of potential buyers, you can build visibility and thus grow your client base. Each time people read your company name and associate it with something positive, it will reinforce their awareness of your brand and help them differentiate your company from your competitor. And last, but not least, PR is excellent for when you enter a new market or launch a new product or service, and you need to alert potential buyers that you're open for business. Effective PR can draw them in and educate them about what you offer.

Building your online media list

The first thing that you want to do when building a PR campaign is make a list of the most desired media outlets that you would like your company or product to be featured in. You should have a list of about 15 media outlets to start with.

Determine the best media outlet contacts

Once you have compiled your list, you need to determine who the best contact is. Here are the best places to start your search:

- Check the masthead, usually on the inside front cover, or on the second page, of each magazine for its list of editors for specific segments of the publication. Which one most closely fits your company? If you are unsure, the managing editor is a great place to start.
- For television news, you want the assignment desk editor
- For daytime shows, you want a segment producer
- For radio, you want the show producer.

Next, you need to gather contact information: contact name, phone and fax numbers, and email address for each outlet. Use the form provided in Figure 12.1 to organize your information.

PR STRATEGY PLANNING FORM

PRINT (can be local, regional, or national newsstand or industry magazines)

	Media Outlet	Contact Name	Contact Email	Contact Phone
1.				
2.				
3.				
4.				
5.				

DAILIES (newspapers)

	Media Outlet	Contact Name	Contact Email	Contact Phone
1.				
2.				

BROADCAST RADIO

	Media Outlet	Contact Name	Contact Email	Contact Phone
1.				
2.				

BROADCAST TELEVISION

	Media Outlet	Contact Name	Contact Email	Contact Phone
1.				
2.				

figure 12.1–PR strategy planning form

TRADE/INDUSTRY NEWSLETTERS OR EBLAST RELEASES			
	Media Outlet	**Contact Name**	**Contact Email**	**Contact Phone**
1.				
2.				

DOT COM BLOG SITES			
	Media Outlet	**Contact Name**	**Contact Email**	**Contact Phone**
1.				
2.				

figure 12.1–PR strategy planning form, continued

Preparing for contact

Now that you have created your list to include contact information, do a little research on each editor or producer. Watch a few minutes of the television show, listen to the radio show, or read one of the editor's articles to get a feel for who you will be talking to and their work.

Another way to prepare is to call the media outlet, and say, "I am hoping that you can help me. I am in the [insert industry here] industry, and I am looking for the name of the person that would cover that beat." ("Beat," in the media world, means "topic," or "subject of interest.") Avoid giving your company's name to the receptionist because they will send you to the advertising department rather than the editor!

Another great way to build relationships with the media is to send out a quick email to your centers of influence—family and friends—and tell them about your plan to build a PR campaign. Ask them if they happen to know anyone at any of these outlets. Your friends and family know more key people than you can imagine!

Continue to add to your list as you find new media outlets, and update your list every 90 days with the most current contact information. A media list gone stale results in zero coverage for your company.

Make sure that you focus on adding the key decision-makers at each outlet to your list. LinkedIn is a great resource for finding professional journalists and segment producers that are high-level, make-it-happen people. With LinkedIn's new search features, you can dive deeper into user data to find contacts that fit your criteria. For example, you can create a search to find contacts with "reporter" as their professional title within a 50-mile radius of your zip code, but if you live in a metropolitan area, your search may result in more than 15,000 contacts. You can easily narrow this search by limiting other fields or adding a keyword like "business" or "features." LinkedIn also lets you save five searches, so you can be alerted to new contacts that join LinkedIn matching your criteria. When searching for media contacts, be sure to add in keywords to locate decision-makers at each media outlet. Some keywords you might use for print media outlets are *managing editor* or *staff writer*. For broadcast media, keywords to search for decision-makers would be *segment producer* or *assignment editor*. Avoid titles like "associate," "columnist," or "contributor," as these are not likely decision-makers.

> Call the media within seven days after sending them a pitch, use this approach to get that feature or something along those lines.

Launching into media contacts

Once your list is complete, get to know the search options and connect with these top media decision-makers on your list.

Connecting with the media on LinkedIn

Figure 12.2 on page 172 contains another script for you to add your uniqueness to, and start reaching out to connect with your media

> ## SCRIPT FOR REACHING OUT TO LINKEDIN MEDIA OUTLET CONTACTS
>
> Hello [insert contact's name],
>
> I specialize in [insert specialties here—no more than two]. If I can be of any help as a contributing/leading authority in this area, you can call on me for quotes, statistics, interviews, and features.
>
> If you do not want to connect, no worries; please do not report my email as spam, simply archive or delete. Otherwise, I look forward to connecting with you on LinkedIn.
>
> Kindly, [insert name here]

figure 12.2–Script for reaching out to LinkedIn media outlet contacts

contacts online. Note that LinkedIn often changes character limits to messages, so you may need to shorten the script a bit.

Connecting with the media on Twitter

One of the best ways to get connected with your media outlets online and build relationships is to locate them via mediaontwitter.com. If you cannot find the specific contact from your list on Twitter, enter the media outlet's name to see if any of the editorial staff happens to be a Tweeter. If so, follow them, and put them in a newly created Media List in your Twitter account so you can just jump on Twitter once a day for a quick 15-minute check on the media's posts, and reply and retweet as needed to build a relationship. Then jump offline and go about your marketing day. It might take a bit to get their attention, but once you do, it is golden. Make sure that you do not pitch them any story ideas or about yourself. If you build a relationship with them by responding to some of their tweets or ReTweeting some of their stuff, they will definitely check you out; it is a given. Be cautious that you don't use too many of one source's Tweets, because you do not want to appear you're stalking your media contacts! Just do a few per week, and you are in. If for some strange, off reason after 30 days, you've got nothing from them, try a few funny posts tagging them, maybe a funny quote or cartoon, etc., and if that doesn't work, then you might want to check other media outlet contacts or simply sit in patience. Be persistent and know that one day soon, the lightly squeaky wheel will eventually be heard. It may take you the better part of nine months before can get a response from a contact at the *Ellen DeGeneres Show*, but it is well worth the wait if you have determined that her audience is your target market.

Finding additional media opportunities on LinkedIn

Now that you are all set by reaching out to the media contacts on your list via LinkedIn, now we need to take this to an even higher level and find even more media connections and opportunities for you. It is no surprise that the media spends most of its day on LinkedIn, because it is a hidden media gold mine. Where are the high-level media contacts? They are in groups and they are lurking in the answers section.

First, take some time and join at least 10 media groups on LinkedIn that have the focus or keyword "media" in it. You can find these groups by going to the group directory section under "Groups" and simply entering the word *media*, then clicking the search button. You will notice that thousands of groups come up; you can then narrow your search results down by using keywords for your industry. When you look for groups to join, some additional keywords that you can use are *editors, broadcast, TV, radio, magazine, segment producers, articles, or features.*

Next, go to the "Answer Questions" area a few times per week and answer questions related to your topic or area of interest. On dozens of occasions the media not only tends to post a lot of questions in this section, but also tends to monitor the answers on questions asked by other people. Why? Because they search questions by keywords when they are researching and looking for facts, statistics, or just more information on a topic. LinkedIn has it all there for them, and their homework is already done. You can receive ongoing features by answering questions in the marketing category in the answer section on LinkedIn. To get to this section, you just need to click on the "more" option on the top tool bar and then drop down to "answers." Another benefit of answering questions is that people can rate your answers, and if they like what you're saying, it helps your expert level and presence on LinkedIn. Make sure that you provide short, to-the-point answers, but make them different and compelling, and something that your competition would not necessarily know, or provide an answer with your technique or approach.

Set a goal to answer between one and three questions per week by searching keywords or by category in the "Answers" section, and ask one to two questions per month on LinkedIn via your contacts (these answers and questions can have the same focus as your top tips.) For example, a social media maven might post a tip sheet, "How to Get Media Placements from Social Networking" in answer to the question "Are you getting media placements off of LinkedIn; if so, would you be willing to share a few secrets?"

Source filing yourself with the media

As you reach out and get to know your new media friends online, take the next step to publicity success and do what is called "source file" yourself with each media outlet. Source filing in the most basic terms is setting yourself up with the media as their go-to source in your industry for quotes, statistics, facts, and yes, even features. It is like having the media file you in their rolodex. Start source filing yourself by reaching out to your new media connections via LinkedIn. Figure 12.3 includes a few scripts for you to make your own and send out to the media. They are desperate for you, waiting for you, and they need you, so make it happen.

SCRIPTS FOR SELF-FILING WITH MEDIA CONTACTS ON LINKEDIN

Hello [insert contact name],

I specialize in [insert specialties here; no more than two]. If I can be of any help as a contributing/leading authority in this area, you can call on me for quotes, statistics, interviews, and features.

If you do not want to connect, no worries; simply archive my email rather than report it as spam. Otherwise, I look forward to connecting with you on LinkedIn.

Kindly, [insert name here]

This script is a long-form script that is used to follow up with a media contact if you have already sent them a previous email or source file request.

Hello [insert contact first name here],

I am reaching out to you today to ask for your consideration in regard to being source filed under the following topic/area of interest for your media outlet [or beat]:

[insert topic/area if interest here]

I will gladly make myself available to you for interviews, quotes, statistics, and case histories as needed. For immediate story and segment deadlines, I can be reached by mobile phone at [insert number here] or via email at [insert email here]. For more information about me, including my portfolio, please visit [insert site or blog here]. My expert profile is listed on my site [or blog] as a PDF.

If you are considering me as a source in my area of expertise, or if you have already source-filed me, would you kindly let me know so I can update my media source list?

Thank you again for your time and consideration.

Kindly, [insert name]

figure 12.3–Scripts for self-filing with media contacts on LinkedIn

WIPEOUT

I have sent press releases and story ideas to the media, but I have not had any bites. What can I do to get even one media outlet to do a story on me or my products/services?

WAVE TIP

Consistency is key with publicity. It is easier to get the media's attention if you can prove that you are already newsworthy. The best way to do this is to get your local paper to do a write up about your success or challenges with your business or career. Because you are a local, it is much easier to get this type of coverage to start. Tie your story angle into a national topic or trend, and you have your first piece of coverage. Most local newspapers have an open pitch-the-editor or planning meeting weekly; call to see if you can get in on the next meeting.

13

ANCHORING ONLINE RELATIONSHIPS

how to set up powerful email marketing journeys

> *The key to promotion is follow-up. When you don't follow up, you lose the "pro," and wind up with just the "motion."*
>
> —UNKNOWN

E mail has come a long way since its original launch in the 1960s as a way for users of a mainframe computer to communicate with each other to a way to connect with millions of people, including your customers. Let's take a look at email marketing and how it can help you grow your business.

Choosing an email marketing platform

The evolution of email marketing has gone from simple one-on-one emails and auto-responders, now referred to as "email 1.0," to a much more sophisticated way of communicating with your customers, "email 2.0." This is a totally new way of doing business where companies or entrepreneurs collect specific data on the

177

behavior of their ideal clients so they can send them more targeted emails that will yield greater results. With advances in technology today entrepreneurs now have the capability to tailor the messages they send to their audience based on their customer's interests, preferences, and purchase history.

With all the capabilities now available in email marketing systems, there are a few basic things that you need to know to build deeper relationships with your customers to increase revenues, grow your business, and set you way ahead of your competition. Email platforms are a must in today's online world of mass messaging, anti-spam laws, and contact list organization. It is now time to focus on getting you set up with an email journey, or if you already have one in place, we need to do a quick SPAM check (sales pitching after meeting) as well as a few other checks to make sure your messaging is powerful and consistent. But first you need to decide which platform is best for your contact management and overall email marketing goals. Explore (and set-up) which email system you would like to use. The top products to date are:

- ConstantContact.com
- Aweber
- Mail Chimp
- 1ShoppingCart
- Exact Target

Infusionsoft and Exact Target offer complete CRM (customer relationship management) capabilities, which include not only database and campaign management but interest, preference, and purchase behaviors so you can tailor your message and campaigns. Other systems such as Mail Chimp, Constant Contact, and Aweber offer more basic email database and campaign management. Decide what capabilities you want and use a check list to compare systems. Most email marketing programs have training and free support to guide you through the learning process. No matter what program you decide on, make sure it includes an analytics system so you know who clicked to open your email and if they clicked on any links that you included inside the email. Additionally, check to make sure that the email program you use does not have a high "blacklist" rate. Features commonly used to filter spam are whitelists and their blacklist counterpart.

Whitelisting is a method used to classify users' email addresses as legitimate ones. Often email addresses that are saved within your address book are automatically considered to be "whitelisted," whereas emails that are considered spam are considered "blacklisted." Email servers can query any commercial blacklists or whitelists to determine if an email's source IP address is present on either list. Once the IP address has been cleared, the email message can be transferred to the recipient's inbox. If the IP address is found on a blacklist then the email can be rejected by refusing the email transmission and terminating the connection.

Calls to action (CTA)

Having an effective "call to action" is an essential part of any web page. A call to action is not just limited to ecommerce sites. Every website should have an objective it wants users to complete, whether it is filling in a contact form, signup for a newsletter, or volunteering their time. A call to action provides

- Engagement
- Valuable, non-sales-bitchy offer
- A sense of urgency or exclusiveness

To create your CTA you need to:

- *Lay the groundwork.* Before a user is willing to complete a call to action they have to recognize the need. Infomercials do this very well. Before they ask people to respond, they first identify a problem and present a product that solves that problem. You also need to communicate the benefits of responding. What will the user get out of completing the call to action?

- *Sweeten the deal.* Offer a little extra to encourage users to complete a call to action. Incentives could include discounts, entry into a competition, or a free gift. This is the approach Barack Obama used on his fund raising website. If you made a donation of $30 or more, you got a free T-shirt. Of course, the beauty of this offer was that not only did he persuade you to donate, he also turned you into an advertising billboard!
- *Have a small number of distinct actions.* It is also important to be focused in your calls to action; too many CTAs will overwhelm the site visitor. Studies have shown that if the shopper is presented with too many varieties, she is less likely to make a purchase. By limiting the number of choices a user has to make, you reduce the amount of mental effort. Effectively you guide the user around the site, step by step. It is not so much the number of actions as the uniqueness of each offer. Here is an example of three quick and to-the-point actions:

1. Create a profile
2. View demo
3. Buy now

Digging into this example deeper, presenting all three on one page creates confusion because the visitor doesn't know whether to create a profile first or if she can just "buy now." A better approach would be to push the buy option later in the process, once the user has committed to creating a profile and a level of trust has been built.

- *Make sure that you use active, urgent language.* A call to action should clearly tell users what you want them to do. They should include active words such as *call, buy, register, subscribe, donate.* All of these encourage the user to take an action. To create a sense of urgency and a need to act now, these words can be used alongside phrases such as: offer expires; for a short time only; order now and receive. When you are running an event or product special, offer an incentive to take action right away and include an action-taking early bird discount. You should do this with all of the events and trainings that you offer. Don't just do it because the urgency approach works; do it because you want to connect with action takers who make things happen that help grow your business in exciting ways.

- *Use white space.* It's not just the position of your call to action that matters; it is also the space around it. The more space around a call to action, the more attention is drawn to it. On the opposite side, if you clutter up your call to action with surrounding content, it will be lost in the overall visuals and noise of the page. Some of the most powerful calls to action are surrounded by white space.

- *Raise the call high.* Another important factor is the position of your call to action on the page. Ideally it should be placed high on the page, and in the central column above what is called the fold of your site, meaning if people have to scroll down to see the offer, you will lose half of the visitors immediately when they land on your site.

- *Fly the right colors.* Switch up the colors on your call to action and test what visually works better for your audience. For example, fast food restaurants tend to use the colors red, yellow, and blue because studies have shown that they insinuate fast as well as prompt hunger. Color is an effective way of drawing attention to elements on page, especially if the rest of the site has a fairly limited visual color palette.

Contrast is also a visually powerful approach to use. By making your site muted by low tones and colors such as blues and grays, you can then make a call to action stand out by placing it in orange. this extreme contrast leaves you in no doubt as to the next thing you should do. Of course, never rely solely on color. Keep in mind that a large number of computer users will not see some color combinations if they are color blind.

- *Size matters*. The size of your call to action is equally important. The bigger your call to action, the more chance it will be noticed. Check this out by browsing the web to see which calls to action stand out most. You will likely notice that you are more likely to not only find but click through the larger ones.

- *Use the call to action site-wide*. Include some type of call to action on every single page of your website, because you never know where some people will enter your site. Don't assume that visitors will land on your homepage. As links to your site begin to build visibility in search results, people wind up landing on your blog, product area, about us page, and even your contact page, especially if they Googled your contact information. A call to action should not just be limited to the homepage. Every page of your site should have some form of call to action that leads the user on, especially if they landed on your contact page—you do not want them to just write down your number and then leave the site. If the user reaches a dead end they will leave without responding to your call. Your call to action does not need to be the same for each page. Instead you can use smaller actions that lead the user towards your ultimate goal.

- *Carry the call through*. Consider what happens when a user does respond to your call to action. The rest of the process needs to be as carefully thought through as the call to action itself. A word of warning: If you require users to provide personal data about themselves, resist the temptation to collect unnecessary information. The less you ask, the more likely they are to provide their information to you. Start with the basics of just name and email. Do not ask for their address, phone (unless you are running mobile campaigns, but it's better to keep a mobile call to action on a separate page.) Marketing people in particular like to build up demographic information. Although valuable, many regard demographic information as personal and asking for it increases the chance that a visitor will drop out of the process. Remember that you need to build trust and that people will connect with you and buy from you only at the level they trust you.

An effective call to action is the number one focus of a successful site and involves bringing together the best practices in usability, visual design, and powerful copy writing. If it is done right it can generate measurable returns and being that we are focused on growing our brand online, that is what the goal should be, a return.

Lead capture

It's easy to set up forms on your site or blog to allow for visitors to give you their contact information such as email, name, and phone number. Choosing the right email marketing software system is a start, but setting up the actual forms throughout your site that automatically capture the visitor information when entered and sends it into your organized email database is vital. Without automation, manually trying to enter, track, and send emails to visitors can become a logistics nightmare. This type of lead capture form can be created on your site by doing what is called "capturing code," and cutting as well as pasting it onto your site. If you have some basic html knowledge, then this is really a no-brainer, but for those of us that would rather have our teeth pulled than learn html, there are thousands of specialists online that can do this in a matter of minutes for you. You can also ask your email software company if they can make it happen as well. Some of them have special packages when you sign up with them to set up your first three call to actions.

The point of having an email capture is to automatically gather and organize the user's information from your site. Once they willingly give you their information, or "opt-in," you then need to have their information organized so you can better communicate with them moving forward. For example, if your call to action offers them something related to tips on how to build their wealth, you would want them to go into a wealth-building campaign database. If they clicked on the call to action that helps them locate investments, then they should automate over to an investment location campaign database.

Email messaging

Even if you have only 10 email addresses, you need to start somewhere. Add them into your email database and begin to build. Once you start a list, make sure that you launch a marketing journey to keep in touch and in front of your contacts without overwhelming their inbox. Send between one and three emails per month, maximum. It's not about the quantity, it is about quality of emails. To help you better manage your email journey, set up what are called auto-send or auto-respond emails. Go into your email program and set up at least six emails that will automatically release on the dates and times you choose to send out to your list. Keep them short, simple, and to-the-point, and do not make them sales bitchy. Use them to educate and build relationships, and the rest will follow. Make sure that each email has several links for more information, because this is how you can gauge their interest and determine how to keep marketing to them.

Remember that your email messages are about the reader. What can you do for them, how can you help them? When you identify this core email message, the next step is to keep it brief and make sure that your email is not 14 pages long. One or two short paragraphs in an email with a catchy subject line can attract the reader's attention from the opening click. If you have something really important that you want them to read or see, including a link with more information that takes them to your blog is an excellent way to get them to check out your site every now and then. Make sure that you mix up your email links with partner blog links here and there as well. If you feel that one of your blogging friends has something of value to add or share with your contacts, go ahead and share their info or blog post; both you and your friend will benefit.

Behavioral email marketing

Part of a 2.0 email marketing approach is to build triggers in the email process that can help you track your prospects' behaviors and interests. Here's an example of a trigger: Sue Client clicks on a link in one of the emails you sent her about your product or service. It automatically sends (or triggers) a message for you to send her information on another product or service based on the links topic (in technical jargon, "triggers" are used to send clients into a new sales cycle based on that link's topic). Think Amazon books and "Today's Recommendations for You." Not only has email technology and software evolved, but the way that we use it to communicate is now shifting how entrepreneurs market and grow their businesses. You can start by adding triggers into your emails that take interested contacts through an "emotion sales" process. For example, if you are selling flowers and your first email educates them on what flowers are in season with the interest of getting the visitor to send flowers to a loved one, you would want to add in several links into your email that will monitor what is called their "click behavior."

This new way of email 2.0 marketing is quickly making its way into business and proving to be an effective way to increase your relationships, response rates, and conversions, through smart, automated communication. All About Spelling, a company that was put to the test using InfusionSoft, one of the leading email 2.0 software companies, doubled their sales in just 90 days by simply learning how to market to their customers by setting up "triggers" in their emails (www. infusionsoft.com/case-studies or www.infusionsoft.com/aas-story).

Monitoring communication campaign results

You need to have at least one time per month where you and your team look at reports to see which of your emails are more effective and have a higher rate of opening, as well as click through. Use those email examples to build your next campaign. It is important to know how your list is responding to the emails that you send. If you aren't getting a good click-through response, it is either your message or the topic. Test a few emails with your top clients or customers to see what they respond to and what they don't. Offer them a discount on services for their time. Again, less is more when it comes to the emails that you send. So what is a low opening rate? Well, that depends on the industry as well as the list you have built. Aim for at least a 50 percent opening rate. If you see that it starts to fall below that, get busy trying new language, messaging, and focuses for the emails that you send out.

Adding a personal touch to every email is important as well. If you are sending the same email out to a massive amount of people, try to use language and messaging that would make the reader feel as though you are only talking to them, by using words such as "you," or directing a question that is geared toward an individual response. For example,

WIPEOUT

I send my clients and customers a newsletter once a month, but I really don't see any sales from it, and it takes a lot of my time to put together. Are these still effective?

WAVE TIP

No. People are too busy nowadays to read about your "news." Do not make something that you send out about you; it needs to be about them and for them. Change it to a customer appreciation or highlight letter. "Why Our Customers Are the Best" or "A Sneak Peak at Our Customer of the Month" will get customers or clients jumping at the chance to be in your "customer letter" every month. Plus, you can get them to provide an overview to you, and this way you do not have to write all of the content. You might have to do some editing though.

"What do you think about . . . ?" Remember that readers will be able to gauge your sincerity as well as whether you are being authentic. If you try to be someone you are not or your brand personality is not incorporated in everything that you send out, you will notice that your opening and click-through rate will be much lower, which means the amount of people opening your email and clicking on links or content that are in the email and actually reading it.

14

CHECKING OUT SOCIAL SHIPS ONLINE

what certain sites are good for, and when you should and shouldn't use them

> *If you don't like something, change it; if you can't change it, change the way you think about it.*
> —MARY ENGELBREIT

Facebook, Twitter, LinkedIn, YouTube, Digg, Stumbleupon—you've heard all the names—in fact you use some of them personally. But when is it right for your business? And what one should you use? This chapter takes you through the list of social ships and helps you figure out what they are good for. Some sites are not for everyone yet others seem to gather and focus on or in certain industries. How do you sift through all of the options. First, in looking at each social site make sure that you take the time to see if your target market is actively on that site yet further more are they engaging in conversations. You might even find prospects looking for your product or service indirectly in the conversations that they are having with others online. For example: "I have had it with my mobile phone, need to search for new one." If you are a mobile phone or service provider this is a great opportunity for you to jump into this conversation and convert this person to your customer. Additionally others just might see the post and support going back and forth and check out what your mobile company is all about. So, how do you find these conversations? You monitor certain keywords such as "mobile phone" and even add in "don't like, hate, can't stand" to monitor deeper conversations. Now that you know what you are looking for on sites, let's dig into some of the top sites individually.

If you can't wait to go motoring over the internet's social waves, you can jump to Figure 14.1 on page 192 to see a condensation of the pros and cons of the top social media sites we're going to check out in this chapter.

Facebook (for networking with friends)

Facebook is great for social interaction as well as getting feedback from customers. Survey or question posting can be very powerful for a brand, especially when you are doing product or services development. This book was built using feedback from Facebook connections about what they thought made a best-selling book. Facebook is an excellent site to drive traffic to your website, as well. The "viral potential" is lower on Facebook compared to other social sites, and Facebook is not as powerful with search engine ranking because of their privacy options when it comes to releasing information on search engines. If you want better search engine results with Facebook, then go into your privacy options and enable the search engine feature.

The Facebook news feed is a great way to stay informed with your social circle, clients, and prospects to see what they are up to. This can be a very powerful marketing as well as communication tool. Even if your connections are scattered across five continents, you can keep up with their lives on Facebook. Why is this important? When you connect with them individually, you will have conversation starters, and if they are a past acquaintance, you feel as if you were never really out of touch with each other. Even your closest friends get a better-rounded picture of you on

Facebook. When you meet your friends offline, you are likely to talk about some topics, but not others, based on what the context of the conversation is. On Facebook, however, you are likely to reveal more sides of your personality and talk about what you are reading, watching, listening to, feeling, or thinking about. So, your friends get to see sides of you they haven't seen before. Remember that friends can be the most powerful referral machines in your circle. They already know you; you have built a trust relationship together. In a nutshell, do not underestimate the power of your friend circle. Facebook is best for networking with past friends as well as building new friend relationships. It is a more personable site where connections can see and read more of you, and vice versa.

Due to Facebook's constantly changing privacy features, you can choose who you want to share with, and what exactly it is that you want to share, making it an excellent platform for personal friends and family connections, as well as prospects and clients. The Facebook privacy settings are the most comprehensive of all social networking platforms and give you granular control of who can see which parts of your profile and activity stream. If you don't want your school classmate to see what you are doing, you can only share a limited profile with him, or even "unfriend" him.

Facebook is great for discovering interesting friends of friends, especially with the new privacy settings. If you and I share a common friend, we are also likely to share at least some common interests. Services like Thread enable you to discover interesting people who are friends of your friends and even let you ask your common friend to make the introduction.

A few features to ♥ about Facebook

- Ask questions to a specific list or friend(s)
- Tagging people that you are connected to in your post so your post goes directly on their wall
- Switching between your fan page and personal page under your personal account

THE SOCIAL COMPARISON CHART

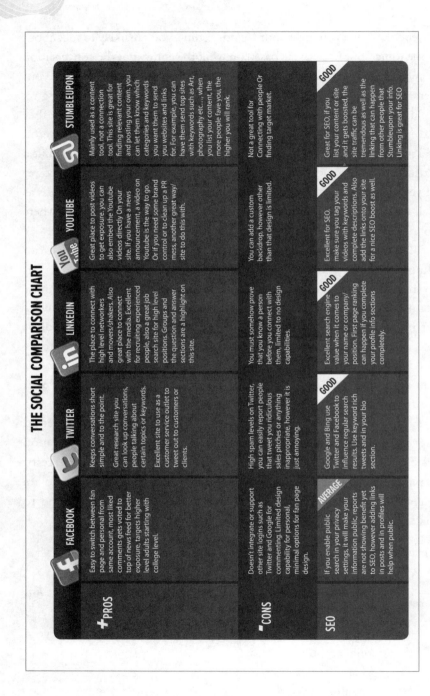

	FACEBOOK	TWITTER	LINKEDIN	YOUTUBE	STUMBLEUPON
+ PROS	Easy to switch between fan page and personal from same account, most liked comments gets voted to top of news feed for better exposure, targets higher level adults starting with college level.	Keeps conversations short simple and to the point. Great research site you can look up conversations, people talking about certain topics or keywords. Excellent site to use as a customer service outlet to tweet out to customers or clients.	The place to connect with high level networkers and movers/shakers. Also great place to connect with the media. Excellent for recruiting experienced people, also a great job search site for high level positions. Groups and the question and answer sections are a highlight on this site.	Great place to post videos to get exposure. you can also embed the Youtube videos directly On your site. If you have a news announcement, a video on Youtube is the way to go. Or if you need some brand control or to clean up a PR mess, another great way/ site to do this with.	Mainly used as a content tool, not a connection tool. This site is great for finding relevant content and posting your own, you can let them know which categories and keywords you want them to send you websites and links for. For example, you can have them send top sites with keywords such as Art, photography etc..., when you list your content, the more people fave you, the higher you will rank.
– CONS	Doesn't integrate or support other site logins such as Twitter and Google for commenting. Limited design capability for personal, minimal options for fan page design.	High spam levels on Twitter, you can easily report people that tweet you ridiculous sales pitches or anything inappropriate, however it is just annoying.	You must somehow prove that you know a person before you connect with them, limited to no design capabilities.	You can add a custom backdrop, however other than that design is limited.	Not a great tool for Connecting with people Or finding target market.
SEO	*AVERAGE* — If you enable public search in your privacy settings, it will make your information public, reports are not showing benefit yet to SEO, however adding links in posts and in profiles will help when public.	*GOOD* — Google and Bing use Twitter and Facebook to influence regular search results. Use keyword rich tweets and in your bio section.	*GOOD* — Excellent search engine value when it comes to your name or company/ position. First page ranking can happen if you complete your profile info sections completely.	*GOOD* — Excellent for SEO, make sure you tag your videos with keywords and complete descriptions. Also add the links onto your site for a nice SEO boost as well.	*GOOD* — Great for SEO, if you list your content or site and it gets boosted, the site traffic can be tremendous as well as the linking that can happen from other people that Stumbleupon your info. Linking is great for SEO

Image designed by Big Fish www.justlikestarrs.com

figure 14.1–Social Sites at a glance

	FACEBOOK	TWITTER	LINKEDIN	YOUTUBE	STUMBLEUPON
LIST BUILDING	*GOOD* — You can separate your friends, clients, college buddies etc... and monitor or post by list.	*GOOD* — You can separate people into lists and view tweets by those lists. For example: family, social media news, clients, etc...	*GOOD* — You can organize your contacts into lists if you upgrade and pay for it.	*AVERAGE* — You can add videos that you like to view or that you have uploaded to your channel to a playlist. For example: videos for clients playlist, funny videos, how to videos etc...	*AVERAGE* — You can organize your stuff by category.
ADVANCED SEARCH FUNCTIONS	*GOOD* — Great way to find new target market connections using keywords that they would use in their conversation.	*GOOD* — Great way to find new target market connections using keywords that they would use in their tweets.	*GOOD* — Yes, half of the advanced functions are free; the other half LinkedIn is now charging for but well worth it so that you can find your target market, key contacts and connect.	*BAD* — No, you can however browse videos by keywords or category to find videos to share with your audience or find out what competition is doing.	*BAD* — No, only basic search for keywords or in categories
ANALYTICS	*AVERAGE* — Yes for fan page, not yet for personal or groups	*AVERAGE* — Only through a social media dashboard such as Hootsuite or Tweetdeck.	*GOOD* — Yes, you can now see your page views and visitors to your services, clicks on any images with links you've added, which industries are interested in your company and even which companies have been looking at your page.	*GOOD* — Yes, you can view insights to see how many views, where views are coming from, demographics and popularity.	*AVERAGE* — You can set up analytics through Google. Directions are at http://www.stumbleupon.com/ads/blog/custom-campaign-tracking/
ADVERTISING PLATFORM	*GOOD* — Yes, great demographics and psychographics, however the ad space is small and limited in design.	*BAD* — Not Yet	*GOOD* — It is newer but already getting positive response and massive traction.	*AVERAGE* — You can promote your video by paying for views, basically they have a pay per click ad model.	*AVERAGE* — Yes, you can pay per visit. Great tool if you aren't getting enough organic traffic.
SAFETY/PRIVACY	*GOOD* — Currently some of the best privacy options of any social site. You can customize who views wall posts, pictures and overall information.	*GOOD* — 2 options, either make your tweets private or make the public, there is no in between	*AVERAGE* — You can make your contacts private and keep your profile public, this is a great feature if you are protecting a portfolio of clients.	*GOOD* — You can make your videos public, private or unlisted which means people can only view it if they come across the link or if you provide it to them.	*BAD* — Basic privacy options, you can block unwanted messages or users from contacting you.

figure 14.1–Social Sites at a glance, continued

Image designed by Big Fish www.justlikestarrs.com

LinkedIn (connecting with high-level networkers)

Mainly used as a social network for business professionals and high-level networking, you can potentially engage customers by encouraging your team members to answer industry-related questions that people post, and become known as an expert in the field. LinkedIn is great for personal branding as well as showing your organization's portfolio. To make your company profile even more powerful, have your team members maintain complete profiles to show off how amazing and talented your team is. LinkedIn has been excellent in helping with search engine optimization, pushing individual, personal names of people with active profiles to the top ranks of search results. As far as site traffic goes, it isn't as consistent as Facebook or as viral as Digg or Twitter, but it's getting better.

You will love how you can utilize LinkedIn to get a hold of people in companies that you'd like to do business with. It's far easier to have a way in when you both know someone in common. You can also keep track of colleagues and clients that change companies. If they change companies or location, your obsolete business card can't match LinkedIn's ability to let you see where they have gone, and keep you in contact—especially if you want to continue to do business with them.

LinkedIn isn't a dynamic site like Facebook where it's easy to have casual conversations with people, or send them quirky links on the spur of the moment. Rather, it's a fairly static site that mainly allows you to:

- host a resume-like profile for yourself;
- have access to similar information about other people;
- show off the fact that you're networking with other people in such-and-such a field.

Another great benefit, of course, is the recommendation feature, where you can have someone write a recommendation for you, so if a prospective employer Googles your name, they'll go to your LinkedIn profile and find your friend's comment about how you are so amazing to work with.

To make it easy for people to message you via LinkedIn, include your email in parentheses next to your username—for instance, Suzie@ suziescompany.com. This way, someone that finds you on LinkedIn and genuinely wants to talk to you doesn't need to worry about how to send you a LinkedIn message—they can just send you a regular email. It is just another way to use LinkedIn as a way to initiate spontaneous conversations. LinkedIn is a really well-focused site if you are of the mind that networking is an important key to your professional/ business success, it's pretty-much becomes the place to be.

A few features to ♥ about LinkedIn

- The "Recommendations" section is an excellent way to build your social proof
- The "Groups." offer a world of opportunity for any business
- The ability to see how connected a profile is so you can link up with high level networkers.

Twitter (engaging with prospects and customers)

Twitter is an excellent communications tool allowing for quick, simple, and to-the-point conversations with prospects and customers. It is a great monitoring site and works well for management of conversations. Twitter is not all about what you have to say; it is more about what you can get others to say about you, or do what is called ReTweet (RT), or "forward" your posts and content. Getting RTs and having ongoing interactions can do more for brand exposure than any other social site. Twitter is an exceptional tool for assisting with traffic generation from other sites like Digg, StumbleUpon, and Facebook. As with Facebook, Twitter isn't very high up there when it comes to search engine optimization and helping with your page ranking.

Twitter really is a community of friends and strangers from around the world sending updates about moments in their lives; yep, that pretty much sums it up. Curious people can make friends, bloggers can use it as a mini-blogging tool, developers can use Twitter's application programming interface (API) to make Twitter tools of their own—the possibilities are endless! So how does this all translate into business? Not only can you use it as a place to have live, interactive conversations, you can also use it as a research and development tool. For example, if you are looking for paid speaking engagements, you can look up keyword conversations using Twitter's advanced search tool to locate meeting planners, corporate events, marketing events, etc.—to find and connect with people who are either in the meeting planning industry, or maybe talking about an upcoming marketing event. You can find dozens of speaking opportunities this way. Think of Twitter like an active, ongoing business mixer that you can jump in and out of at any time and have a conversation with any of the people who are following you or that you are following.

A few things to ♥ about Twitter

- Creating lists so you can view Tweets by certain people in your news feed
- It is a great monitoring tool to stay informed about what people are saying about you or your industry online
- It's an amazing research tool, with advanced search options that will help you find any opportunity you want, whenever you want.

YouTube (exposure and brand control)

YouTube is still one of the hottest video sites on the internet and is now known as a top search engine online. People are starting to research companies' reputations by visiting YouTube to check their channel and/or videos. Make sure that your videos and messaging are consistent and in line with your brand when posting on YouTube or any video channel. When you tag your videos with powerful keywords concentrate on your branding and industry focus, YouTube is an excellent source for search engine ranking. Video is widely becoming known as a great tool to use to do reputation repair, as well as to do question-and-answer quick clips or respond to customer complaints.

Seeing an adorable baby saying things that even adults shouldn't be saying on YouTube.com has its giggle value. But what some people don't realize are the practical reasons to utilize one of the greatest resources available to the public. Need to know how to tie a tie, right now? YouTube is an excellent and quick resource when you need to get this right, and fast. Thanks to the advent of YouTube, late-bloomers who never learned this skill can go online and see a step-by-step video tutorial on how to tie a plethora of different types of knots. The person who posted the video had made it part of his branding, which he promoted by offering a valuable how-to for his customers and potential buyers.

YouTube is also an exposure outlet. Think about how many people have become famous for doing idiotic things and posting them on the internet, as compared to legitimately trained actors and actresses who have based their lives on trying to become famous. It's coming to a point where being famous is as easy as catching a candid moment on tape, and not being embarrassed of your boss or prospects possibly seeing it.

A few things to ♥ about YouTube

- The feature that allows videos to be embedded directly onto a website
- Setting options to make videos public or private
- You can assign a vanity name as your own channel user name for more powerful branding

StumbleUpon (content recommendation engine)

StumbleUpon is not a communications social site; it is more of a content engine. The "Paid Discovery" option can be good for brand awareness because you can target your message very accurately, but keep in mind you will pay $.05 per visit ($50 CPM—cost per 1,000 impressions). It is a good thing if your story makes it to the top page for its tag, and when that happens, you might get hundreds of thousands, even millions, of visitors. Due to StumbleUpon's large user base, many people can find your stories and link to them. Stumbleupon is getting better for search engine ranking, especially when your site or story gets main stage.

StumbleUpon, hereafter referred to as SU, is one of the social websites that was started with a vision of allowing users to find what they are looking for with the help of ratings provided by scores of other users. Based on the recommendations of users, SU helps you find the right content, be it web pages, videos, photos, or sites which otherwise could have been difficult using a search engine. In the internet lingo, it is best known as a recommendation engine as opposed to a search engine.

If used effectively, SU is an excellent internet marketing tool that can assist an individual or a company in growing their business. A few benefits of SU are increased traffic by helping you increase the footprint of your site to the entire world. In order to make this happen, you have to get your site in the SU system by listing it and encourage readers/visitors to start rating it. The more thumbs up you get, the better, because it means users like your site, posts, videos, photos, etc., which attracts others and translates into increased traffic to your site.

SU can also help you boost your page rank. This is done through backlinks. When you have many visitors providing links to your site from their own site, it adds a point to increase your site's page rank. With increased page rank, your site now becomes visible to the world when users enter keywords that match your site's contents into the search engine. This ultimately will help you bring more traffic to your site, which leads to greater exposure for your products and/or services to the masses.

One of the greatest features of SU is that it allows you to analyze and visualize your site's incoming traffic. This information is crucial to any marketer, because it helps in understanding visitors' surfing habits on the site. Research shown via SU has the lowest bounce rate, meaning few users leave immediately after landing on your site. Because SU is a recommendation engine that is virtually run by its massive user base, SU is just like word of mouth.

A few things to ♥ about StumbleUpon

- You can choose to have SU email you top sites, content, videos, etc., related to your keywords and industry.
- It is a great word-of-mouth tool for valuable content.
- The possibilities of one of your content pieces becoming viral via this site's traffic are awesome.

Digg (content discovery and delivery)

Digg is not a site used for customer interaction, but a content engine where you can post your stories, tips, videos, etc., and see if people "Digg" it. The more Diggs you get, the more exposure is possible. You might even end up on a Digg's front page story. Brands have an opportunity to gain mass exposure on Digg, particularly through stories posted about your company. It is a site for content discovery and delivery. Digg seems to be one of the most consistent viral-traffic generation sites that can send tens of thousands of visitors to an individual post in a matter of hours. Even if your story doesn't become popular, it will still get your page indexed very quickly. Also, if your story does become popular, this is likely the best site in terms of getting the attention of bloggers who will link to you—a great way to build blog partner relationships.

The long-term benefit is bigger and undervalued when it comes to sites like Digg. More people are starting to use alternatives to Google to find stuff on the web, hence the popularity of sites such as Digg and SU. According to a post on Digg, "61 percent of Digg visitors go to posts older than a month, 37 percent go to posts from this month, and 12 percent go to current news.

A few things to ♥ about Digg

- Using it as a research tool when looking for facts or statistics
- The content is often better in regard to being relevant and more recent, compared to what you find on Google
- It is easy to navigate and customize your account for an even better user experience

WordPress (website or blog base to use as your foundation online and post content)

WordPress is an open source content management system (CMS), which in English means you can openly and easily make changes to the site. Often used as a blog publishing application, it has many features including "themes," a template system using a template processor. Users can re-arrange widgets without editing any code; they can also install and switch between themes. WordPress also features integrated link management, is search engine-friendly, and has supports for tagging posts and articles.

We'll spend a little extra time here in the WordPress section because you will love its capabilities and easy-to-use features. First of all, the fact that WordPress is free to use just makes it rock all together. One need not be tech-savvy on codes in order to start blogging. The WordPress software does the coding for you so even a kid can start blogging. OK, maybe a kid isn't a great reference, being that most kids can pass up adult html and technology skills in a matter of just a few minutes! The point is, all you have to do is write something down and hit the "publish" button. What makes it even more attractive is the fact that WordPress sites are pretty darn spam resistant. If spam bugs you, you need not worry, since WordPress has a strong system to combat it. It uses the well-known Askimet, the best spam blocker in the world today. In fact, it is so effective that it can block around a thousand spam comments on some WordPress bloggers daily. Should the system be infiltrated by spam, it can easily be reported to be kept away and off the system.

WordPress is amazing for search engine optimization and Google seems to love WordPress-powered sites. Time and again, they tend to rank easier quicker and stronger than other software platforms. Combining Worpdress with a great search engine optimization program increases your chances of having strong, natural rankings within the search engines. WordPress continues to offer new plug-ins that automate search engine optimization for your site. A favorite SEO is Scribe (scribeseo.com), where, for a minimal monthly fee, you can have your keywords automatically updated and incorporated onto your site.

The fact that WordPress is easy to install and customize makes switching to it a no-brainer. (Was that convincing enough to make you switch your website to a WordPress based site?) The themes used to present your content are easy to change and because it is open source software, users all over the globe are designing new themes every minute that can be used to put the color and creativity in your blog site to reflect your personality or the nature of your business. You can also categorize and even tag your posts at the time you are writing them. Your post can be categorized by date and category, which makes browsing your blog or site easier. Categorizing your blogs also improves search engine optimization results since the same topics are grouped together. It is also a good way to organize entries for easier management and archiving. To boost your posts even further, users in the WordPress community have engineered thousands of plug-ins that are also available for installing on your blog site. They are intended to customize the blog according to the desired purpose of the blogger, and some provide powerful business solutions such as ecommerce and subscription modules, usually free of charge.

A few things to ♥ about WordPress

- The privacy options: you can create a completely public blog site, or a private one that only members can access, or a per-post password option, which is an occasional private entry in a public blog. It is a wonderful membership-based tool as well.

- The Blog Talk feature—you get to receive comments and feed-backs automatically from the readers who, at their option, may post them to your blog. You also have the option to control who and who cannot comment in your blog.
- Thank goodness for the spell-check editor that makes writing easier. That is all that needs to be said here!

Tumblr (blog meets content engine)

The ability to ask and answer questions makes this site a potential darling for customer communications. Tumblr has a very simple platform and excellent ability for content sharing, making this a great branding tool. Images can get traffic on your Tumblr site, as well. Currently almost all activity happens directly on Tumblr itself, and they also rank very well with the search engines.

When you consider using Tumblr for your blog, there are a series of potentially compelling benefits that might be of interest, depending on the kind of site you wish to run. By using bookmarklets, mobile apps, phone posting, IM submissions, and other tools to post content, it is very fast and very easy to get short-form content onto your Tumblelog, including video, images, quotes, etc.

And with Tumblr you can choose a theme as a starting point but customize it with almost limitless potential. This includes adding advertisements and a custom domain name.

A Tumblelog is hosted on Tumblr's service, which has proved capable of withstanding large traffic spikes and being generally very reliable. Tumblr is completely free, with no need to pay for any features or tools. Some of the drawbacks with Tumblr are that it can be bad for long posts; the longer the posts you plan on making, the worse Tumblr performs. Not only are the templates designed for shorter posts, the lack of auto-saved drafts and no "MORE" tag equivalent (at least not without additional work) to show only part of the post on the front page, make it poor for longer posts. Currently there are no plug-ins available to add directly to the HTML code. Tumblr doesn't come with a built-in commenting system, and you'll have to turn to a hosted solution, such as Disqus, to make it work. These solutions often don't fit in well or look natural. Finally, if you use a self-hosted solution, you can always pack up and move your blog, take your database with you, etc. With Tumblr, you're at the mercy of the company. Though there are ways to export Tumblr blogs, the process is much more complicated than many hosted solutions. All in all, the advantage of a Tumblelog is that it is easy to create, set up, and run. It requires little time and maintenance to keep going, and can reach a very large internal community. However, those who demand total control over their site will likely be wary of Tumblr's requirements and limitations.

A few things to ♥ about Tumblr

- The Tumblr feature wherein readers with their own Tumblr blog can simple "tumble" your post over to their blog for more exposure
- It is pretty darn easy to use and navigate
- The traffic potential from Tumblrs can be huge, if your content rocks, which it will after reading this book.

Squidoo (mini blog to create niche pages or publish wen pages on your favorite things)

Squidoo is just one of the many new innovative web 2.0 methods to get some extra traffic to your web pages. They have search engine power with Google as well, and their pages rank very easily on top. If you link to their pages a few times, you'll boost the chance that page will rank in their top ten. If you link to relevant article web pages, you'll get a boost from having a juicy, relevant link with the text you're going after rankings for. You can also create your very own "lens" page to help establish you as an expert, and you can donate the AdSense or other earnings from your lens to charity, or take a percentage for yourself.

A few things to ♥ about Squidoo

- You can upload affiliate partners to a lens such as Amazon or eBay.
- You can put everything together all on one page for one topic: links, resources, books, other tips and lenses. It is a very powerful way of blog posting on a highly traffic site.
- It is beyond easy to use: you can create a lens in just a few minutes.

WIPEOUT

I would rather get my teeth pulled than get on Twitter and Tweet! Do I really need to be on this site? It seems like it is a waste of my time.

WAVE TIP

Simple answer: No, you do not need to be on Twitter. Let's avoid the root canal, though, and quickly review why you should strongly consider it. Twitter is like attending a live event any time you want. It is a way to meet new people, find opportunities, and connect with the media. If you do not want any of these, then stay off of Twitter. Remember, however, that it takes more time to go to a local networking event nowadays than it does to jump on the live Twitter feed and have a dozen or so conversations.

15

ONLINE HIDDEN TREASURES

top sites and resources that you might not know about

> *Winning isn't everything, but wanting to win is.*
> —VINCE LOMBARDI

Amazing resources abound for you to check out and consider. These tried and true hidden treasures are divided into sections for video, your website, and social sites. Let's do this!

Video resources

- *Pixability.com.* This site has a plethora of video marketing tools, as well as a free online video grader to tell you what you are doing right and where you can improve with your video creation, marketing, and posting efforts. They offer free and paid-for services. Their site is easy to use and has a ton of resources to enhance your video marketing knowledge.

- *KillerSalesVideo.com*. Although this is a one-man show run by Chris Willow, he uses templates that he created to put together a pretty amazing intro for your site for around $50. He does have higher-end packages, but his $50 intros are certifiably effective, garnering hundreds of views, and a ton of positive feedback. His average turn-around is 24 hours. Simply provide the copy and chose one of his video templates, and you, too will come to love outsourcing and can forget about taking three months to learn videography!

Website and blog resources

- *TheHelloBar.com*. This is a top bar tab that can be added to your site as a simple notification bar that delivers your message and can drive more clicks. Some top users are Timothy Ferris, author of *The Four Hour Work Week*, and Gary Vaynerchuk, author of *Crush*. An amazing way to use TheHelloBar was demonstrated during the 2011 earthquake and tsunami in Japan, when sites used it to encourage donations and volunteers to join in the rescue and recovery efforts.
- *Yahoo! Explorer*. This site is a great way to check people and sites that are linking to your site. It is also a great way to keep track of who is linking to your competitors' sites—it is time to start building relationships with those peeps. This is a free service offered by Yahoo!; however, they will make you set up an email account to access this benefit. It is totally worth it.
- *Add Share Buttons to Your Site or Blog*. Empower your visitors to publish and share your content because if visitors like what they read, they will promote you without being asked. Make it easy for them to do by adding a share button. Make sure that you do the same in return, and find out what content is shared more often than others. Go to www.addthis.com/bookmark.php and grab the code to add to your site.

- *Websitegrader.com*. Check to see how your site looks in Google's eyes, basically. Websitegrader will tell you if your site rocks or not. Check this every so often, as they constantly update what they are analyzing in regard to your site. Do not get overwhelmed if your site error list is a mile long. Just take a few things at a time and fix them. In this ongoing process, you may find for periods of time that when you check your site with Websitegrader, something might be off; at least it brings it to your attention.

- *TemplateMonsters.com*. You can search through thousands of free and paid-for WordPress site templates to use and/or customize your WordPress blog or site. You will love being able to search by category or artist on this site. Although there are thousands to choose from, you can usually find what you are looking for in the first few searches.

- *Planbookedu.com*. Now this site is way cool! A free tool to help you get yourself organized, it mainly focuses on getting your lesson plans organized. Try it for your own personal organization—you'll love it.

- *Tungle.me*. This is an auto-scheduler that will sync with your Outlook and Mac calendars. Finally, a place where you can send potential clients and customers to chose a time they would like to chat or meet and pencil it in! You then get a notification, verify that the time works for you, and boom! You are scheduled on all calendars.

Social site resources

- *Honestly.com*. is a professional reputation and peer review website—kind of like a mix between LinkedIn and Yelp—with community-contributed reviews of individual business professionals. Because consumers are increasingly turning to the advice of others when it comes to making purchase decisions (big or small), review sites will gain solid traction over the next few years. This is one thing that's overlooked in the online space—a review site where people can look up professional reputations about people they may want to work or partner with, or even discuss business.

- *Yobongo.com.* This is a cool site to chat with people nearby. Now there is a concept: Get to know people in your community. If you are a brick and mortar, this is an excellent way for you to reach out and connect in your community with people who are active online. Offer them a cup of coffee at your coffee place or a free copy at your copy center—OK, maybe 10 free copies, but you get the picture.

- *Threddie.com.* You're going to wonder where this site has been all your life. This is a site where you can brainstorm, get ideas, and share ideas to help people out in an online forum community. So, if you are feeling stuck, your ideas are boring you or your partner, do not fear Threddie is here.

- *Sprouter.com.* A great connection site for startups to network and collaborate between entrepreneurs globally, Sprouter provides a platform for users to connect with other innovators. Entrepreneurs can expand their networks to include fellow entrepreneurs and startups with similar interests and goals.

- *Company.com.* This site is somewhat similar to LinkedIn, however it seems to have more internal networking capabilities where you can share information and connections with co-workers and vendors. It has a free 60-day trial period; after that, there is a paid-for option. It is worth checking out to see if any potential prospects are on the site that you should start to reach out and connect with.

- *Quora.* A simple site where you can ask and answer questions, as well as search by topic or area of interest, this is an excellent research and development tool. Who knows? You might even meet some new people on this site and start to build relationships with them.

15 / online hidden treasures

- *Weeplaces.com.* A fascinating research tool for location and buying behaviors, this site provides a little map to show you all of the places that you have checked into. You do know that location-based marketing is going to be the next black, right?

- *Appsplit.* OK, are you ready to create your own mobile app? This company specializes in the business of mobile apps and provides a marketplace where individuals and businesses can buy and sell apps. If you are looking for an alternative to completely relinquishing ownership, you can participate in a Split Program where you can take on the responsibility of managing and marketing applications on behalf of the owner in return for a percentage of the profit.

- *Backupify* (http://secure.backupify.com/). Another great site that offers free backup of your online contacts, because you never know when Facebook and Twitter might get hacked and/or crash. OK, so the chances of that happening are pretty slim but still, it is good to know that your contacts are safe and sound online, should you need to retrieve them.

  To stay informed on Facebook changes in regard to their website, their team, and their mission focus, visit www.insidefacebook.com/.

- *Plancast.com.* This is a simple site to use and look at. Jump on and find or list events that you are attending, or would like to attend, by category. Oh, you are so social now, look at you go!

- *Go2web20.net.* On this amazing site you can find new sites to help enhance your marketing efforts, monitoring, or just make life and business a bit more fun. Offering resources and explanation for sites such as Food Journal, where can you create your own food blog, to Pen.io where you can become your own online publisher. Be careful though, you could get stuck on this site for days!

- *Etsy.com.* Whoa, this site is way cool to not only shop on, but, hello! Get set up with a store and sell cool things that you don't want anymore—just in case you needed more money to invest in your marketing. Before you go on, put your credit card down and back away from the shopping cart area.

- *Endor.se*. This site helps people connect through friendly recommendations. When you post a recommendation for someone here and use their Twitter name, it will automatically let them know that you posted a recommendation for them. What a cool way to send a little word gift!

- *Dapsem.com*. Thank friends, clients, customers, and/or cheer them on, using this site. It is a strange name but they seem to be stuck with dapsem-ing people; it will eventually stick everywhere else. Hey, did you go dapsem someone today?

Search engine optimization

Now, with all those resources to choose from, let's step aside for the rest of this chapter and take a brief overview and update on search engine optimization (SEO). One of the most important things to have in place for any SEO-focused marketing is your list of keywords. This list is not a one-time creation; it is an ongoing, must-be-updated-monthly list because your keywords will always be changing. In order to create this list, let's quickly review what is referred to as "The Short Tail and Long Tail of Keywords." The keyword space, when it comes to what are called short-tail keywords, is more competitive and harder, as well as more expensive to break into. Examples of short-tail keywords for a shoe manufacturer are *shoes, flat shoes, women's shoes, footwear*. The corresponding long-tail keywords might be *Cushioned flats, stylish yellow by Clarks*. (See Figure 15.1.)

Focusing on your long-tail keywords, use the form in Figure 15.2 on page 212 to help identify your keywords for SEO. Use these words in your blog post, on the front homepage and the inside pages of your site or blog. In addition, use them with all of your social networking posts and interactions, when applicable. An important thing to remember in

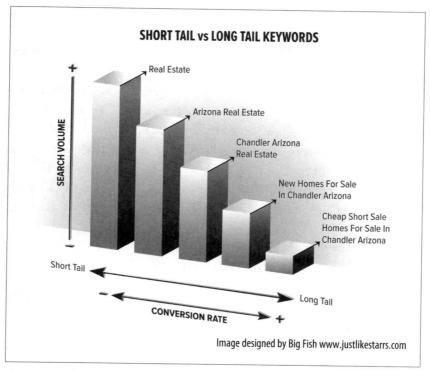

figure 15.1–Short tail vs. long tail keywords

building your keywords list is that it takes some creative brainstorming, effort, and more importantly, time and patience in changing them up to see what works and what doesn't. However, those who take the time to create keywords with a clear goal almost always generate better results than those who do not.

Who is your ideal client or customer? This is the essence of your keywords: Ask yourself:

- *What do they do for a living?* Are they a homemaker, waitress, CEO, buyer?
- *What is their spending range for your product or service?* Ex: they most likely budget for this type of product and studies show. . . yes,

you read that correctly—go do some research online and see what studies say about your industry by typing in keywords!

- *Where will you find them online?* On Facebook, Yelp, Foursquare, Twitter, professional forums?
- If *they were to search for your product or service online, or if they were to call information, what keywords would they use to describe what they are looking for?* A yellow pair of flats, size 6, open-toed shoes?
- *What is the need that you are going to fill for them?* Make their feet feel better with comfortable, cushioned flats; have the shoes in any color to match anything in their wardrobe; price the shoes in their budget range between $50 and $150 per month?

KEYWORD TEMPLATE

Questions to ask yourself in creating your keywords:

1. What does my client do for a living?

   _____

2. What is their spending range?

   _____

3. Where will I find them online?

   _____

   BONUS: What keywords would they enter to find my product or service?

   _____

   BONUS: What need will I fill for them if they purchase my product or service?

   _____

---

figure 15.2–Keyword template

You can also make it easy for your visitors to social bookmark your website, creating important links that the search engines value. There are plenty of free social bookmarking widgets available via Digg, Delicious, StumbleUpon, and Squidoo, just to name a few. For more sites simply Google search "social bookmarking sites." Widgets are small applications that can be installed and executed within a web page by an end user. When you see a Twitter feed directly on a homepage site, you are looking at a widget.

Here are a few more ways that you can boost your SEO results for your brand.

- *Have multiple domain names.* If you have several topics that could each support their own website, it might be worth having multiple domains. Search engines usually list only one page per domain for any given search, and you might warrant two. In addition, directories usually accept only homepages, so you can get more directory listings this way as well.

- *List your company URL with search engine directories.* After you've gone through the search engine optimization process, it's time to get your site listed in the various search engines and directories. You can start by submitting your site using a free submit form. Some of the major search engines and most of the smaller search engines will provide a form that you can use to submit your site for free. With the smaller, or thematic search engines, this is a good method to use. For each search engine you'll just need to locate the "submit URL" form and submit your homepage. There is no need to submit anything else. And, you don't need to keep submitting your site month after month. Re-submitting your site over and over after it has been indexed does nothing but waste your time. It will not improve your rank in any way.

Don't be surprised when you find that not all of the major search engines even provide a free submission form any more. With the major search engines, submitting your site isn't even necessary. This is because the major search engines will find your site through links to your site from other sites and this is why it is very important to begin getting incoming links to your site as soon as possible. You should start by getting your site listed in the major directories.

The best way to be sure your site is found is by submitting to the major directories that are crawled by the search engines. This is a good approach for the search engines to take because sites listed in directories have already been reviewed by an editor and been considered to be worth a listing. When you are submitting to directories, be sure to take the time to find the best category for your site and read the submission guidelines provided by each directory. By following their guidelines, you will improve your chances of being listed and decrease the amount of time it takes to get listed. Obviously, there are many directories where you can submit your site. Here is a reference site to get you started: www.searchengineguide.com/searchengines.html.

After you've submitted to these directories, then you can begin submitting to other directories, you can find current directories by simply searching on Google under "search engine directories." It will take time for the search engines to index your site, after it has been listed in the major directories. So, be patient, and expect to wait at least a couple more months before your site starts appearing in the index of the major search engines.

- *Create articles and publish them to ezine sites, or ask to be included in a vendor's ezine or online newsletter.* The links stay live often for many years in their archives.
- *Avoid Flash on your site.* Flash might look pretty, but it does nothing for your SEO. If you absolutely must have your main page as a splash page that is all Flash, or one big image, place text and navigation links below the image or Flash intro.

- *Link your site through quality sites.* The quickest way to get your site spidered and indexed is by getting a link to it through another quality site.
- *Check your server for blacklisting.* If you are on a shared server (check with your web team or host), do a blacklist check to be sure you're not on a proxy (a proxy server is a computer system or an application program that acts as an intermediary for requests from clients seeking resources from other servers) with a spammer or banned site. Their negative notoriety could affect your own rankings.
- *Have a call to action.* Here it is again, but you must know that SEO is useless if you have a weak or non-existent call to action. Make

SweetSearch is an excellent search engine site just for students, so if students are your target focus, get on there. If they aren't yet, get on anyway, check out conversations, and see where you can fit in. Students are a huge market. Don't leave them out of your target reach.

sure your call to action is clear and present. Go back and re-read the CTA section in Chapter 13 to make sure that you not only get this but that you implement it right away.

Location-based marketing

Location-based sites are not something to take lightly. Imagine checking in at an airport, and shortly thereafter receiving a connection from one of your online friends that they were there as well. You might end up taking the opportunity of a flight delay to have a few drinks and get to know your contact on a more personal, in-person level. Your conversations from that event might even help each other out with a few projects.

This new marketing beast not only opens you to new possibilities when it comes to meeting your online friends, it allows you to target-market relative to location and buying behaviors. Don't avoid this amazing and still-untapped resource.

If you are cautious about who you choose to meet online, you shouldn't have much to be concerned about when it comes to meeting people in person. However, always be smart about your in-person meeting choices.

Starbucks is using location-based check-ins to their advantage, and their customers love it. As soon as someone checks in to a Starbucks using sites such as Four Square, Starbucks will send them a coupon special with an offering of some sort. This is not only a great way to entice a purchase; it is a brilliant way to gather your market's buying behavior, as well as location behavior, also known as "infographics." Location check-in is hitting smart phones around the globe and Yelp has even added location-based check-in to their application, so you can check in at a place that you are reviewing and post about the experience at the same time.

Here are a few sites for you to check out and dabble in the location world:

- Foursquare
- Facebook Places
- Gowalla
- Loopt
- BrightKite—on this site you can share locations with friends and connections via text. Whoa!

Because Facebook Places is so new, let's take a really quick tour here and learn how to check into Facebook. Go to touch.facebook.com and login with your Facebook login information. This site was built primarily for tablets and touch-screen computers, but it also works great on desktops, laptops, and in any smartphone browser. Once logged in to Facebook, look for the status update box (the box that says "What's on your mind?") and click the "places" icon on the right. You will then be prompted, at the top of the page, to allow Facebook to use your current location. If you want to add your page to Facebook Places, you have to allow the application to do so.

Next, you need to search for your organization from your organization's location. Whether it is on your desktop at work, or a laptop on location, Facebook will generate your organization's exact location and plot it on a map, so you need to make sure you search for your organization while on location. If your organization already has a Places Page, it will show up in the list. If not, you will be prompted to add your organization. Add your page and spell out the name exactly as you would like it to appear, insert a brief description, and then click "Add." This will then create a Facebook Place page for your business. Now you can go click "Like" on your new Facebook Places page.

When you are done with that, look for the link at the bottom of your new Places page that says "Is this your business?" Click it. You will then see a pop-up that tells you that claiming the place will turn it into a Facebook page, allowing you to post updates to people who like the page, update your business information, and more. Places can only be claimed by official representatives. After you click "Proceed with Verification," you will need to enter an address and phone number, and provide one of the following by selecting and uploading your articles of incorporation, business license, or Better Business Bureau Accreditation.

If you are concerned about privacy but want to use Facebook Places, then take some time to read about its privacy features. If you want keep your friends from tagging you in their Facebook Places check-ins, go into the "Facebook Privacy Settings" menu and check the options so only you can post your location on Facebook.

WIPEOUT

I can't seem to keep up with all of the new technology and resources. It seems like every time I get one thing, 100 other shiny new sites or resources have just surfaced. How do I make sure I am always using the most current tools without having to read an ongoing feed of updates 24 hours a day?

WAVE TIP

There are several great sites that can keep you informed yet not overwhelmed. Mashable.com is great for social media sites, and you can check out technique updates at Techcrunch.com for new technology. Just spend an hour every week to read through the latest and greatest. What you need to know will magically appear; at least that how things seem to work!

16

CUSTOMIZE YOUR SOCIAL SHIP

top sites that you can customize to
create a better customer and brand experience

> To think is easy.
> To act is difficult.
> To act as one thinks is
> the most difficult.
> —Johann Wolfgang
> von Goethe

There are a ton of new ways to customize your profiles on social sites so that they look exactly the way you want them and provide a variety of business solutions. Customization is extremely important for not only your company brand image but for consistency when marketing online. If your Twitter profile looks different from your Facebook profile you can cause confusion with your branding. Let's look at each of your social sites in depth to make sure that you are consisten with your brand image and your overall marketing on each site.

Facebook is more than social

Facebook customization for fan pages can turn a page into a purchasing platform. A rapidly increasing number of businesses are adding an option to use the social networking site to browse and buy their products. Furthermore, you can use your fan page to run contests, encourage brand word of mouth, and get together with connections in a branded space. Let's first take a look at a few customization options to have your storefront on Facebook:

Facebook storefront customization options

Payvment—www.facebook.com/payvment

This free beta (as of publication of this book) app allows you to handle your entire e-commerce operation through Facebook. You can accept credit card and PayPal payments, which are credited to your PayPal account. You can customize charges for shipping and choose whether to charge sales tax. Unless you disable the option, your products will also appear in searches people make on other Payvment storefronts when they choose to search "all of Facebook."

Other helpful features include selling multiple quantities of an item from one listing; the ability to give discounts to customers who like your page; and adding options like sizes or colors to item listings. Store owners have access to their selling histories and order statuses, and they are able to send messages to buyers through the app. Implementing Payvment's instant payment notification can help keep on top of orders as they're made. This is becoming a very robust system for Facebook fan page storefronts.

Storefront Social—http://storefrontsocial.com

This storefront shopping cart software creates a tab on your page that allows you to showcase items in your online store. Some templates include options to Tweet or share specific items, and shoppers can search by customizable categories or with a search bar. In order to set the store up, you need to install the Storefront Social app. The basic package costs $9.95 per month. You cannot use the store as your sole storefront because there is no way to complete a transaction using the platform. Rather, people who wish to buy your products are directed to the product URL that you provide. If you are a seller on eBay or Amazon, you could link to your listings on those sites, as well.

BigCommerce SocialShop—www.bigcommerce.com/socialshop.php

Like Storefront Social, BigCommerce SocialShop doesn't allow transactions. It directs users interested in products to an online store and allows them to share their products on their walls. Because BigCommerce is a full e-commerce platform, it's a more extensive Facebook storefront tab option. At $24.99 per month for the most basic package, it's also the most expensive.

Ecwid—www.ecwid.com/demo-frontend.html

This app allows customers to drag and drop products into a shopping bag and check out without leaving Facebook. You can integrate the same store on your website, MySpace profile, LinkedIn profile, or Tumblr, by copying and pasting widget code. Basic accounts are free, but selling more than 100 items will cost you $17 per month.

A great website for designing your own Facebook fan page customization for little to no cost is Wix.com at www.wix.com/upgrade/fb-app-showcase.

You can also customize your tabs on Facebook and add in video as well as custom graphics, banners and landing pages; this does require FBML knowledge (Facebook markup language). There are hundreds of people online who specialize in FBML so you don't have to. They will create your custom fan page starting at $97. The really great customized fan pages can cost thousands, but the cost is well worth it if you have a brand you want to set apart from your competition.

Customize Twitter

A custom Twitter background can make a positive impression and enhance your brand, but how do you make one? You can start with the basics by using one of Twitter's 12 stock backgrounds. Each background has preset colors for the elements on the page. You can also modify the colors of the overall background, text, links, sidebar background, and the sidebar border. The first thing you should do is get that generic background off of your Twitter account, unless, of course, you like branding Twitter without getting paid for it, and do not like standing out, then fine, just leave it. However, the fact that you are reading this book shows you want more, so let's switch your background and change the color palette. All you need to do is go to "Settings" in the top row of links on your Twitter page, click on the "Design" tab, and then either select a "theme," or click on "Change background image," or "Change design colors," and get creative. Don't worry about messing anything up, because any changes you make will not be visible to anyone but you until you click "save."

You may be perfectly happy with one of the themes Twitter has provided for you but there are still going to be thousands of people on Twitter with the same background as yours. It's like having the same company name as a bunch of other—well—companies. The best way to make sure that your Twitter page doesn't look like anyone else's is to upload your own background image. Those of you with the necessary skills might want to use Photoshop or a similar program to create your own from scratch. If that's not a possibility, then there are other options. You can simply upload a photograph you've taken or even your logo and choose the tile option to just tile it onto your background. The image will tile (repeat) in an appealing way. You can also search Google for "tile background" and you'll find thousands of places to get them if you do not have a logo or one of your own.

ColourLovers.com is an excellent place to start if you want to make your own tiling background patterns. They also offer palettes that help you pick colors that go well together so your Twitter page doesn't look like you picked the colors with your eyes closed or let your parrot do it for you. What, don't people still have parrots? TwitterPatterns.com is another great place to find patterns for your tiled background.

Another way to create a unique background is to use a photograph. There are a few things you'll want to keep in mind, though. For one thing, a limited amount of the photograph will actually be visible. Realistically you have about an inch on either side of the main text area to work with. That means if you upload a cool picture and you are in the center of the photograph, no one is going to see you.

If you want the photo to fill the entire background, the size of the image is also important. Twitter will give you their current picture file size specs when you go to upload your photo. Once you've selected your background, you may want to change the colors of the sidebar background and border so they complement the colors in the overall background image. Don't pick a dark color, or your text will be hard to read. You might be tempted to use white or light-colored type on a dark background, but if you use light colors for your text links, they won't show up in the upper row of navigation links.

Your Twitter background can actually work for you like a business card if you use the space on the left side and, to an extent, up to the top. A professional-looking Twitter background also makes an excellent first impression and will help you pick up followers who might have otherwise overlooked you. Even if someone only looks at your profile one time, the results could end up being well worth the time and effort you put into creating an attention-getting background.

A custom Twitter background gives you the opportunity to tell someone more about what you do aside from the 160-character limited bio you get to put in your sidebar. An obvious choice would be to use your logo along with a bit of text, perhaps something like: "Mention you saw us on Twitter and. . ." insert your offer. If you don't offer a product, but just want to promote your blog, you might want to use design elements from your website and then add a bit of text about your blog, along with the URL and your email address. A custom background is also a good way to let people know at a glance what company you represent, which is especially important if your company is well-known. For example, Zappos CEO Tony Hsieh has a Twitter page with over

30,000 followers, but word has it that nearly 300 Zappos employees also have Twitter pages as part of the company's marketing plan. Since only one Twitter page can use the domain twitter.com/zappos, the best way for the employees of Zappos to let people instantly know what company they are with would be to use a custom background with the Zappos logo on it somewhere.

LinkedIn customization

By simply adding applications and widgets to your profile, you can create a different experience for your profile visitors. You might find yourself saying, "Who needs a website anymore? Just use a social profile!" Applications on LinkedIn do many things, from adding your WordPress blog feed or your Amazon Suggested Reading List, there is also a Company Buzz widget that will populate a Twitter feed of anything that is mentioned using the keywords that you entered when setting it up. These features can be added from your edit profile button at the top of the navigation bar. These are great ways to automatically show your connections what you've been up to. The 15 applications that you can add through the "Add Sections" link are as follows:

Applications
1. Creative Portfolio Display
2. Events
3. FT Press Delivers
4. Google Presentation
5. Huddle Workspaces
6. Lawyer Ratings
7. Legal Updates
8. My Travel
9. Polls
10. Projects and Teamspaces
11. Reading List by Amazon
12. Real Estate Pro

13. SAP Community Bio
14. SlideShare Presentations
15. WordPress

In addition to all of those fancy applications, LinkedIn recently added a "personalize your profile with patents, publications, and more" option located in the "edit" section of your profile. The five new sections that are now available for you to use within your profile are "Publications," "Certificates," "Languages," "Skills," and "Patents," the last of which is very important and pertinent to our country's quest for technological advances and innovation. The Publication section now allows you to add your original, published works to your profile. Share with your connections specific publications that will help showcase your areas of expertise. The Certifications section gives you the ability to list any certifications, clearances, and licensure that you have attained throughout your professional career. Not everyone will have the ability to add to this section. But think of it this way: in your profession or industry, are there a lot of others who do what you do within your own geographical area? For those who have certifications, licensure, or special clearances, this section will help you build your credibility and help you stand out in the crowd.

The Languages section tells what languages you are fluent in. If you are fluent in more than one language, or are even somewhat proficient in another language, this section allows you to share this information with your connections. The Skills section can be added to your LinkedIn profile to show what skill sets you have and what your areas of expertise are. You can either type in your own skill sets or type in the first letter or two to populate a list of skills that start with that letter. You can then choose your level of proficiency for each skill, as well as choose the number of years of experience you have for each skill. Other than the skill itself, there is no requirement to choose a proficiency level or set number of years, but by choosing a proficiency level for each of your skills, you set up realistic expectations. You would not want to be skipped over because your profile does not exude proficiency, but you also do not want to inflate your experience and tell people you are more proficient than you are in a given area. It won't take long before people will know the truth. And last but not least, the Patent section: What better way to show prospective venture capitalists, competitors, and consumers what patents your company has been issued or applications you have pending?

In addition to adding new sections and applications to your profile, you also have the ability to reorder the sections on your profile using the site's built-in drag-and-drop technology. This enhancement was added as a result of it being one of the most highly requested profile features from LinkedIn users. This feature gives you the ability to highlight the skills, expertise, and/or experiences that you would like to portray first and foremost. To do this, simply go to the section you wish to move, place your curser along the top of the section, then drag and drop it to its new location within your profile.

Customize YouTube channel

There are three simple places where you can customize the look and experience for the user on your YouTube channel: channel info, channel design, and video organization. For your channel info, make sure that you take some time to fill in and complete all of the sections such as description and tags, as this information is indexed by search engines. Your channel design is the most important option of all. This is where you can specify the colors of your page or specify a background design. You can also rearrange the layout of the boxes on your page, specify which video will show at the top of your page, and much more. Many users may choose to have a default plain color on their page but you can also upload a customized backdrop or wallpaper as your background to make your social sites reflect your brand. Just upload your wallpaper in the "advanced design customization" section, choose "repeat background image," and bingo! You've got yourself a nice, branded background. You can change the font, the playlists that are displayed, the boxes that are displayed, the color of the links, and the color of the text as well. When it comes to organizing your videos, you can choose which uploaded video shows up first or in a certain order. So if you have a video that you would like to display more prominently, you can bring it forward.

No matter how you decide to approach your social site customization, it just needs to be done. If you want to show that you are serious online, that you are a brand to be recognized and remembered, then invest time and/or money to make this happen. You will feel better about your online brand and so will your prospects and customers.

WIPEOUT

I do not know html or website coding to do customization, yet I do not have the budget to outsource. What can I do to make my social sites look presentable with my branding without having to learn code or break the bank?

WAVE TIP

Customization is not as expensive as it used to be because there are so many people online and around the world who do it. If you truly cannot budget $100 for some customization, then you can just upload your logo and tile it on sites such as Twitter or Youtube. For Facebook, you can upload your logo as the profile picture file. You should, however, find a way to budget customization and get it done right, because your brand image online is your client's first impression. Check out sites such as custom-page.com that sell a wide selection of ready-to-go templates.

NAVIGATING THE SOCIAL OCEAN

create a well-rounded online social marketing plan

> *If you don't know where you are going, you'll end up someplace else.*
> —YOGI BERRA

If you do not have a plan and take action with the tips, templates, scripts and techniques in this book, none of it matters. You might as well donate this book to your local library. So let's focus on creating a well-rounded online social marketing plan that will get you results from your efforts.

Setting goals and mapping plan

First you need to set some solid goals. A few examples of goals are:

- Obtain 500 new emails and leads per month
- Grow my social proof by getting 10 new testimonials per month
- Get two media features per month

- Land a column in a magazine or blog
- Grow my fan base by 250 per month

Next you need to make sure that you have a map or plan on how you are going to achieve these goals. Without a map or a plan it is like trying to go from California to New York without a GPS. You won't know what routes to take, the approximate time it will take to get you there, and the vehicle(s) that you are going to use to get there. Here are a few quick questions to help you move your plan forward:

1. *What vehicles are you going to use?* Social sites, video marketing, email marketing, blog? List the top three vehicles to get started with. You do not need to overwhelm yourself and choose every single site covered in this book; just choose a few and have at it, go all the way, or as they say, go home. Dig your heels in and stay there.

2. *How often will you move forward in this plan, meaning, how often will you blog, post, and search for key contacts and target market online?* Determine what that is and write it down, add it into your schedule, if you have to. If you are delegating this to a team member, make sure that she gets the proper training to build and execute your online marketing plan.

Create an action list

Now let's focus on the action items that you need to create within your plan to get to your goals. Here they are listed in order of action priority for your journey online:

1. *Set up a general and accessible email address for your use throughout the online world, e.g.: social@xyzcompany.com.* It is easier to keep emails separate for each brand/company journey that you are managing. If you are working for a client, you will need web-mail access link and password information.

2. *Create a keyword list for your campaign or client.* You can pull top keywords from Google analytics or use www.wordtracker.com

3. *Create your policies and procedures.* Make sure that you tell team members and all involved what they can and cannot do when it comes to posting on behalf, or about your brand online. If you are working for a client, determine if there are any restrictions in regard to posting on social networks. For example, some companies do not want employees talking about their brand online under a personal profile; this is usually spelled out in the company's employee manual. If you are posting on a client's behalf, determine from the client if they want you to clearly identify that you are posting on their behalf. For example, you or your client may prefer wording like, "Check out top tips on how to lose 7 pounds in seven days: click here—posted by VA Susan Smith on behalf of [client name]"

4. *Set up monitors and social accounts.* After you get your main social accounts set up, get your computer decked out with a social media dashboard such as Hootsuite.com or Tweetdeck.com. If you are working for a company with an IT department, you may need to arrange to have these installed on the mainframe. Once these are set, make sure you go to google.com/alerts to set company and competition alerts for you to monitor.

5. *Set or change all site passwords for easy access.* If you are working on behalf of a client, use company-assigned email address for user name, and set the password to initials for the campaign or client and 4 random numbers such as 7795, e.g. starr7795 (note: it is easier if you keep password all lowercase, if possible).

6. *Run a social check report using sites such as www.socialmention.com to see where your brand or client is at online.* Keep the results on file and run this monthly to compare.

7. *Power up social sites and blogs by customizing their design and checking the copy, as well as visual balance, on each site.* Make sure that all sections on your social profiles are 100 percent complete.

8. *Create your content and find a place or system as to where you can keep or store it for easy access so that you as well as anyone on your team*

can have access to it. This would be for your top tips, articles, reference sites, blog partners' content links, etc. You can use programs like BaseCamp.com or ACT, or you can simply keep it all in a Word or Excel document and post on Google docs or docstoc.com.

9. *Set up analytics.* Whether it is Google analytics (google.com/analytics) or Open Tracker (opentracker.net), you need to set up analytics for your site and blog, or you will not be able to monitor your progress and see what is working and what is not. Mashable released a great article on Top 50 Analytics for web traffic; check it out at http://mashable.com/2009/01/12/track-online-traffic/

10. *Set up automation if if you want posts to automatically go out at certain times.* Set up a one- to three-month post automation cycle so you can focus on other social marketing tasks and not have to worry about getting posts out x number of times per day. However, with that said, you do need to engage with people as your posts go out. The point here is that they get sent out/posted, but do not automate and leave them hanging online. You would be better off not posting at all if you are not going to be there to engage with your following.

11. *Create your call to action offer.* This could be one of your top tips, a free report, a video series, access to your membership club for 30 days, etc. Whatever it is, make sure it is a free offering and that it is valuable, saving your clients and prospects time and money, or making their lives or business easier or more profitable.

12. *Set up your email capture and systems throughout your website or blog.* Make sure that you have a specific place where people can give you their contact information throughout your site, not just on your "Contact" or "About" page.

13. *Set a referral system in place.* What about all of the people that love you already? These are people with whom you have either done business, or who highly recommend you. Do you have a

referral plan in place? If not, now is the time to make it happen. It can be as simple as setting up a thank-you card, sending flowers, chocolates, wine, etc. when you receive referrals.

14. *Implement an ongoing communication system.* You need to set up a consistent communication plan with your prospects, as well as your current customers and clients. Set your email foundations, meaning your core email messages, for the next 6 months. Even if you go in later to add to or change, at least the foundation has already been built.

15. *Start engaging in group discussions.* Aside from postings, content creation, and status updates, it is imperative that you engage online in discussion groups at least once or twice a week to help put your name out there and create opportunity. You never know who will be in the discussion and what they might be looking for in regard to your services and products. Make sure this is in your ongoing plan.

16. *Do a product and services check.* Are your offerings and products current? Do they need to be looked at, revised? Does some life need to be added back into them? If a company uses the same product look or service rate sheet for 20 years, chances are they will suffering from stale branding and the resulting dwindling customer base.

Learning systems

Once you have your goals, map, and actions set, you need to make an ongoing commitment to building your skills as well as those of anyone who works for or with you. Without skill and knowledge growth, your brand can be left behind. What is your commitment? Weekly, daily, monthly, quarterly? Annually would be too small a commitment. Education is all over the internet, so whether you take 20 minutes a day to search how-to videos or read an industry update, you need to stay informed and you need to put that same expectation on your team.

Information keeps marketing journeys motivated, fresh, and energized. There is a great illustration that explains this concept:

> Once upon a time, a very strong woodcutter asked for a job with a timber merchant, and he got it. The pay was really good, and so were the work conditions. For that reason, the woodcutter was determined to do his best. His boss gave him an axe and showed him the area where he was supposed to work.
>
> The first day, the woodcutter brought in 18 trees, and of course his boss congratulated him. Motivated by his boss' words, the woodcutter tried harder the next day, but he could only bring in 15 trees. The third day he tried even harder, but he could only bring in 10 trees. Day after day he was bringing in fewer and fewer trees.
>
> The woodcutter thought he was losing his strength, and he went to the boss and apologized, saying that he couldn't understand what was going on. His boss then asked, "When was the last time you sharpened your axe?" Appalled by the question, the woodcutter harshly replied, "Sharpen my axe? I have no time to do that. I've been busy cutting trees."

So the question is: Are you too busy chopping trees on the front line and not allocating the time needed to sharpen your marketing skills? What is that costing you and your business? Furthermore, how much time would it really take to keep your marketing axe sharp?

Here are a few tips and resources to help you sharpen your marketing axe in 15 minutes a day or less:

- Go to sites such as Technorati or the Tweetdeck Directory to find blogs and content links that will take you directly to marketing conversations and resources. Technorati is the hub for top blogs around the globe; you can find any blog topic you want. Tweetdeck, organized by industry or topic, has an excellent directory filled with people posting (aka Tweeting) resources and how-to information.

- Read a minimum of 15 minutes per day, set number of chapters from a marketing book, or get out of the office and take a walk to the local bookstore, and sit on the floor in the marketing aisle browsing through books. You'll be amazed at the marketing concepts you'll come across in the aisle of a Barnes & Noble.
- Search for webinars or teleseminars online from marketing-focused sites and personalities. There are thousands of great webinars and quick-tip videos from marketing gurus and most of them are free.
- Get on video sites and start searching for valuable new how-to approaches using keywords for your industry or topic area of focus. You will be amazed at what type of videos you can find. TED videos are highly motivating and very informative.
- Check in every now and then at Mashable.com. This site is information overload! However, you can stay informed and learn most any social site or internet marketing topic in a matter of 15 minutes.

WIPEOUT

I can't seem to get organized just using a Word or Excel document for my planning. Are there any other programs to get my social media marketing organized?

WAVE TIP

There are a ton of sites that offer social media marketing organization. The better ones, such as Radian6, do have a fee. Roost.com is not only a great site for organizing your social media marketing campaign, it also helps you find more targeted prospects online.

18

MAKE SOME WAVES IN YOUR INDUSTRY

top strategies on how to use
social media for your specific industry

> To open a business is
> easy; to keep it open
> is an art.
> —CHINESE PROVERB

In this chapter we will examine some
useful tips and techniques for those of you working in specific
industries that might have issues dealing with disclosures and
confidentiality, such as law, finance, and health. Here we go.

Financial planners

Financial planning is a tough industry when it comes to online
posting and building a reputation, but there is a way to still engage
and kick some major financial industry butt online. One of the
restrictions in the finance industry is that you cannot ask or post
testimonials for public viewing. So this pretty much slams the
concept of building social proof. "Pretty much" means there is still
room for movement here. Simply positioning this another way (and
always check with legal advisors before doing this), you could ask

your financial planner clients to present or speak to groups and/or organizations and then get testimonials in regard to their presentation of the information and speaking style. It works every time! Here are the top five things you can do as a financial planner to make some magic happen online.

1. *Post in your status box using more of your personality.* Share more of you and your thoughts. People like to relate personally to the people that they hire as financial consultants. They want to know that their financial planners are real people. Do not sales bitch rates, investment opportunities, or what you did for other clients—that is a no-no! You will build your presence online by being more transparent (yet professional).

2. *Hold a free teleconference once per month and invite prospects or even clients.* This is a great way to give prospects and target market contacts a sneak peek into what you can do for them. If you are too nervous to hold your first few calls, just have someone interview you for the first 20 minutes, and then turn it into a Q&A discussion so you can help callers for the remaining 20 minutes.

3. *Offer a free 15-minute assessment of their situation or business and give them two different solutions that they can put into place right away.* This is a great offer that you can post online, starting at your website or even a Facebook fan page.

4. *Share your personal successes*, and not your clients, by posting things such as, "I love it when my income or investments keep increasing," or "I checked out a new place to put some of my moola today, feeling great about the decision because I am that good!" (Yes, you can show off just a little, especially in a joking way, poking fun at yourself but never at others, of course!)

5. *Post industry specific stats and what is happening in the financial world* specific to your niche, but take out your industry lingo and put it into English. If you aren't sure if you are talking in another language online, ask, "Did that make sense?" or "What do you think about that?"

Real estate

Although real estate doesn't necessarily have as many restrictions, there are a massive amount of Realtors® (don't forget that trademark!) online and off. However, most real estate agents and brokers aren't sure how to build their reputation online, or they have no idea what to say and how to say it. Yes, this could apply to most anyone in any industry, but it happens more often in real estate because it is difficult to stop a career habit of pitching properties with photos and MLS (Multiple Listing Service) links. These people have prided themselves in being online since desktops could first access the Internet and have been using it primarily as a sales tool for a very long time? The social wave requires a more side-ways approach. Here are top five tips for Realtors®, brokers, and agents around the globe. Have at it, own it, be consistent!

1. *You have to, must do, no excuses, utilize video instead of copy.* Tell more of a story about a listing or a deal just closed. Forget the static pictures and copy—boring! Instead, put some life into real estate and do a quick, 60-second clip on why a listing is great for the neighborhood, or on the opposite side of that, do a video about what keeps a listing from selling. Be transparent and truthful. Do these updates daily. It will take you five minutes every morning to record and upload online.

2. *Host live real estate community video broadcasts once per month.* Even if you only have your mother show up to the first one (hey, some of us have been there!), just do it. Get in the habit of hosting monthly live broadcasts where you talk about the real estate community. You can focus on a topic for the month such as "commercial real estate or property management—the things you need to know about who is handling your investment. The opportunities with this are endless, and hosting it from your home office or even an outside, onsite location will save you tons of money on renting space, providing food and beverages, etc. You could even invite people around your dinner table to talk real estate. Get the camera up while you are eating with

your family, ad have them join you in a "Let's Talk Real Estate Around the Dinner Table" video series. This could be a great education piece for kids at the table too, get them understanding the importance of real estate investment at an early age, ask them questions, and get them involved.

3. *Pay-per-click campaigns have been extremely successful in the real estate industry when done correctly.* Find a trustworthy pay-per-click specialist (or call/email for a referral—see About the Author in the back of this book) and set a monthly budget to run targeted, pay-per-click campaigns that can bring leads right to your estep (that means doorstep in online lingo).

4. *Get your office involved.* Whether you are an agent within an office or the designated broker, you should get your office involved with some online marketing fun. Partner up with another agent and do some back and forth video or blog posts to get a few different perspectives on the community and local industry. You can specialize in one topic and have another agent specialize in another, for example, you might assign "Buyer Specialist" and "Seller Specialist," or "Property Management Specialist" titles to appropriate team members. There is plenty of business for everyone, even in real estate. You just need to get out there and grab it, even if it is collaborating with another agent.

5. *Write blog posts for community online outlets.* This is a great way to get more exposure in your community and build your credibility. Pete Baldwin, (PeteBaldwin.com) set out to do just that. Within six weeks, he had a consistent column in the most popular real estate outlet online in Scottsdale, Arizona. He is still killing it online to this day!

Medical

Patient confidentiality is a serious issue when it comes to the medical field, and being that the online ocean is public, how do you represent a medical practice, hospital, or individual practitioner and not cross the line? Well, actually, it is quite simple. You can use it as a patient communication center.

1. *Tweet surgery updates.* At first read, that might not sound very appealing, but hospitals are starting to do this. Utilizing Twitter as a teaching tool, as well as a marketing tool, some are Tweeting each step along the way of a surgery. You do not have to use the patient's name; you could always give the patient a pretend name. There is a networking website called Sermo that is exclusive to physicians, and offers a unique, confidential environment where physicians can informally consult on medical cases and share valuable information. This can help you build a personal brand within your industry, as well as your credibility and recognition.

2. *Communicate with patients.* Twitter could be used for scheduling appointments, appointment reminders, practice updates, or public health notifications. Of course, you would want to get signed patient permission to Tweet them about an appointment, but surprisingly, this approach is starting to make waves in the industry. While patients are in treatment or surgery, you can also Tweet their wellbeing updates to their relatives. By using simple messaging such as, "Patient is doing fine," or "Patient is resting" family members who can't make it to a location will feel more at ease.

3. *Make medical statistics more positive.* Do not post the doom and gloom; we get that at every turn. Instead, report on the positive discoveries or happenings in your specialty, give hope, give the good news. The bad news can be communicated privately; online social sites are not the place to do that. You can also do these updates as videos to make them more powerful for the viewer and helps them get to know you more personally and connect at a deeper level.

Government

This is a community where people not only need to be careful what they post about government divisions and information, but also in how representatives respond to the public. There is an excellent site for anyone in the government field to check out and become a member of called GovLoop.com. This site has over 40,000 government representatives across the world. There are some great tips and resources on this site, however, read on to find additional tips for working with government agencies. As always, check with your government appointment legal division as every area is different in regard to what is allowed and what is not.

1. *Post your office updates.* Instead of letting all of our government secrets out online, post about some fun office happenings. This can make politics fun and add a personal element to the government office you represent. Remember you are actually representing you, not just the government so post respectfully. Get creative and post video updates or office party clips.

2. *Post your standards for comments on your blog or social site.* You can post this on your info tab area or bio section. Posting your standards doesn't necessarily mean people will read them, but it still makes it public and helps keep you and your team members in check if you review and delete content according to your standards.

3. *Set up a group in Facebook.* Government can bring people together who are employees with those who are interested in a facet of an agency's work and information. Doing so expands the government's outreach capabilities and ability to interact. You can also use these groups for recruitment. Employees could form groups on social networking sites to overcome road blocks within organizations. For example, if an organization does not allow the employees to post publicly on social profiles about anything work related or direct conversation about that organization, private groups are a great way to connect with other people in the industry or in that specific organization.

4. *Use social sites to engage the public in discussions.* You can start conversations and provide news and tips about government service. You can recruit through posting, as well. The CIA has used Facebook to invite students to apply to work at the agency.

5. *Allow comments on photos.* The Library of Congress' Photostream in Flickr is a good example of posting the government's public domain photos on a social networking site where the public can comment on the photos. This is a great way to get people involved, commenting and connecting.

Attorneys/legal

In this industry, there is great caution regarding what is posted due to client-attorney privilege as well as establishing a client-attorney relationship. Because most legal professionals know what they can and can't post as far as messaging, we'll skip over that and head straight to a few tips on how to build a legal brand online.

1. *Turn laws into light conversation.* Without giving legal advice, of course, this is an excellent way to get people to connect with you on a deeper level. So many people get overwhelmed by the legal talk that they tend to shut down because they are confused. Remember that confusion equals "no" in most situations. So post explanations of legal terms, approaches, and laws in plain English. You can be the legal translator. Make sure that you include your legal disclosures in a sidebar.

2. *Produce legal videos and updates.* This is a great way to provide an overview on a legal topic without giving legal advice. Keep these brief and to the point, under one minute. Make sure at the end of the video to add your website URL and always end by asking the viewer a question. For example: "Have you checked your will lately to make sure that you are covered in this area?" or "Does your house title have the proper ownership noted and legally documented?"

No matter what industry you are in, there is always something of concern when it comes to online marketing and being social. Just do what you would do in person: Be professional, have fun, be respectful, and you will be just fine. Think about the online networking just as you would in-person networking. The only difference is that it is done through a computer or mobile device, not in person. It is still somewhat face-to-face if you consider video and pictures are faces. Well, they are, aren't they? In addition, "do the different" to stand out. Different separates brands and individuals no matter what industry you are in. It is also important that you reinvent your brand every six months. If you start getting bored with you, so will your clients and target market. Whenever you find youself sleeping in a little bit, ask yourself if you are getting bored with your branding and offerings. If the answer is yes, excite yourself, reinvent! Add new energy, new offerings, an updated brand image, and *voilà*, you are connected with your market, ongoing.

WIPEOUT

I have been online now for three months and I have not seen much of a return. How long does it take before I start to see some results in sales and website traffic from my efforts online?

WAVE TIP

It depends on what actions you are taking online and how consistent you are. It takes a minimum of three months, with consistent posting and engaging as well as reaching out five to six days per week. It can often take another three months before you can start to see social conversion to revenue or website traffic increase. Every business is different, but out of any situation you get what you put into it.

19

VICTORIES AND SHIPWRECKS

case studies of what does and does not work online

> People seldom improve when they have no other model but themselves to copy.
> —OLIVER GOLDSMITH

I have searched high and low online and off to find success stories with social media also known as victories and social marketing gone wrong in which I am referring to as shipwrecks. I have also reached out to friends online and shared client successes in this section as well. The point is, be careful what you ask for, yet don't be afraid to get yourself out there online. Let's start with the shipwrecks first.

Mac-and-cheese shipwreck

Kraft Foods decided to play on an old game for a marketing approach and utilize Twitter to deliver and grow the message and outreach to get people talking about macaroni and cheese. The details to their social game went something like this: Anytime two people individually use the phrase "mac and cheese" in a Tweet, they would each get a link pointing out the "Mac and Jinx." The first one to click the link and give Kraft his or her address received five free boxes of Kraft's macaroni and cheese, and a T-shirt.

This is a modern update of the game where whenever two people said something at the same time, you'd blurt out, "Jinx, buy me a Coke." Kraft's campaign replaced the soda with "mac and cheese" for their new "Mac and Jinx" Twitter campaign. According to Mashable, Kraft had developed a new game to get the phrase "mac and cheese" trending on the social networking site. This all sounds creative, right? And they did get some great results and attention for this campaign, but this campaign seemed to take a turn and shipwrecked.

As their campaign grew momentum, it seemed that "mac and cheese" started to trend a topic on Twitter, and when you clicked on the topic, you would see Tweets like this:

Kraft confesses, "we use genetically engineered bovine growth hormone" #food (link to the mac and cheese press release here)

or what about this Tweet from someone famous—Alyssa Milano, who has 1,403,372 followers, posted this Tweet:

"If you buy/eat any Kraft products, please read (link inserted with information about Kraft's food process).

Then from this Tweet followed another one from @WootLive,

"wonder why Kraft wants you to tweet about mac and cheese? It's to bury the news that they use GMO bovine growth hormone in their "food."

This shipwreck has made some people permanently lose their appetite for mac and cheese. If you allow random people the opportunity to Tweet your keywords, be prepared to do damage control if any of your company's less-than-shining moments get sung to the internet ocean.

Dr. Pepper and that porn video shipwreck

A marketing agency won the Dr. Pepper UK account from Coca Cola and started out with a good idea by developing a Facebook application that gave consumers the chance to win £1,000 if they allowed the brand to take control of their status updates. It launched in May as part of Dr. Pepper's "What's the Worst That Could Happen?" campaign. The status updates were randomly generated and ranged in degrees of embarrassment. The worst unfortunately did happen however, as one particularly offensive update ended up on the profile of a 14-year-old girl. It read, "I watched 2 girls 1 cup and felt hungry afterwards." If you're not familiar with it, *2 Girls 1 Cup* is possibly one of the most notorious internet porn videos out there and understandably the girl's mother (who happened to be on Mumsnet.com) was rather upset to find her daughter searching online for the clip to see what it was. The campaign was pulled immediately and the marketing agency was left with some real explaining to do, and a reputation for being out of control and untrustworthy.

OK, really—how do big box marketing agencies get these accounts, and furthermore, who in the world in these agencies actually approved this concept? It is truly mind blowing.

Toyota shipwreck

Toyota marketing created some kind of off-the-wall alternate reality game, whose foundation was that you were being stalked by an unhinged criminal who sent you threatening emails saying that he was coming to your house, backed up by things like MySpace profiles, and even angry bills from hotels he trashed on the way, having given your name as the payment contact. A woman didn't realize that these were a marketing prank and thought she was being stalked, got scared, lived her life in fear, and then sued. Toyota's defense? The woman had taken some online survey in which the fine print gave them permission to send her "marketing and other communications." Make sure your marketing is transparent so your audience understands your message.

Habitat shipwreck

Habitat, an interior design brand from the United Kingdom, made the decision to use the Twitter hashtag functionality to drive users to its products. The manner in which it was executed, however, turned out to be a high-profile, epic fail. The intern given the responsibility for tweeting exploited the controversy over the Iranian election by using the hashtags #iranianelection and #mousavi, which was not well-received by Twitter users. Habitat was accused of piggy-backing on popular topics to market their products, and clearly did not take time to understand their chosen medium and the rules of engagement, or the responsibility that goes with speaking in the voice of your brand.

This story drives the point home that you have got to have your social media policies and procedures in place to tell representatives what they can and cannot do online. Why would you want to tie your brand in with a controversial, political topic, anyway? That is branding suicide.

Murphy-Goode wine doesn't pick a winner—another shipwreck

Murphy-Goode Winery thought they had a clever idea to promote their wines to a younger, internet-savvy audience. They decided to do what they referred to as a "star-search" for a new "spokesperson," and call them a "lifestyle correspondent," using the power of the internet to select the winner, build awareness, buzz, and of course the ultimate goal—goodwill. Applicants were asked to create and post a video to YouTube, explaining why they would make the best candidate. Murphy-Goode encouraged fans to vote on their favorites, and the winery promised to first select 50 finalists, bringing the top ten up to Healdsburg for a final set of interviews.

Over 2,000 people applied, and more than 900 videos applications were posted on YouTube. Thousands of votes were cast, with ex-TechTV and Revision3 host Martin Sargent the clear winner. His submission received 6,600 votes, more than three times as many as the second place video, and more votes than the next four or five candidates combined. But when the winery finally announced their top 50 candidates, Sargent was conspicuously absent from the list. Across the web, it quickly got ugly. First Sargent's fans started lambasting the Murphy-Goode Winery, and then his influential friends picked up on the injustice. Popular web host Leo Laporte told his 136,000 listeners about the travesty, as did Digg founder Kevin Rose (who has 1,061,379 Twitter followers to date). Kevin followed that up by spending nearly 10 minutes talking about the issue with his co-host Alex Albrecht on the popular Revision3 show, Diggnation. The story ended up getting nearly 2,400 Diggs, which was enough to put it into the top 10, where it was seen by a significant fraction of the site's 39 million monthly unique visitors.

There was more negative chatter around the internet—a lot more. And instead of improving the winery's perception among internet-savvy drinkers, the opposite appears to be true. Search for "Murphy Goode" on Google, and you'll find two of the top ten results are negative stories about the failed campaign, with headlines that say "Murphy-Goode's job contest turns sour," and "Murphy-Goode says #1 spot isn't good enough to make top 50." And nearly a third of the 122,000 search results for Murphy Goode are, in fact, negative stories spawned by the Martin Sargent debacle.

If you run a brand video contest, you must be publicly honest and transparent about posting results especially when the video views were posted publicly.

DKNY shipwreck

The People for the Ethical Treatment of Animals (PETA) staged an anti-fur protest on clothing brand DKNY's Facebook fan page. Thirteen different users changed their Facebook profile photos to block letters and posted in quick succession on the DKNY's Page to spell out the words "DK Bunny Butcher" in protest of the brand's use of rabbit fur. Dozens of supporters have since taken to the page to voice their disdain for the LVMH-owned company's practices, reaching many of the page's 200,000+ fans in the process. In addition to the Facebook protest, PETA has also held demonstrations outside of Donna Karan's New York offices and events she has hosted, as well as retail outlets carrying her design. Surprisingly, the posts are still up.

Makeover salon victory

When co-owners Matt Buchan and Alex Garcia decided to buy and make over a hair salon in Seattle, Washington, which they renamed Emerson Salon after Ralph Waldo Emerson, they decided that the internet would be an important focus for their business. Little did they know that two years later, 75 percent of their business would be sourced from Facebook, Twitter, and their blog. Their social branding is apparent from the second that you hit their website. They have links to all of their social profiles, links to all of their stylists' social profiles, their blog feed, and a button where users can book their next hair appointment online. Even more impressively, after booking an appointment, a user can share their appointment with friends on Twitter or Facebook. Since introducing social media into the mix, traffic to their website has more than tripled.

Liberty Bay Books victory

For Suzanne Droppert, the owner of this independent bookstore located in Poulsbo, Washington, that specializes in Scandinavian and nautical books, social media seemed to be a natural outlet because she was already known as a thought leader. Droppert began experimenting with social media after attending an educational seminar early last year. The presenter absolutely insisted the attendees join Twitter immediately. Droppert believes it is important to stay connected with online social conversations regarding your business' space. She stays abreast on books, travel, food, and local events via her store's Facebook and Twitter pages. She also uses the company blog and YouTube channel to keep the community up-to-date on book signings and in-store events on.

In the end, Droppert's goal is to share views, ideas, and conversation with her customers and the authors who visit her store. Her social media efforts, which are an extension of her genuine interest in her customers, led to a growth in sales, as well as a growth in genuine connections with her customers.

Whole Foods victory turned shipwreck

Whole Foods has had an extremely active presence with social media from day one. They embraced all of the top social sites, with over 1.2 million followers on Twitter and more than 100,000 fans on Facebook. There is no doubt that Whole Foods has benefited from its active presence in social media. Unfortunately, years after building a strong following and interaction outlet, Whole Foods has seen a more negative example of the power and influence of consumers using social media.

John McKey, Whole Foods chief executive officer, voiced his opinion about President Obama's healthcare reform initiatives. His comments were published in *The Wall Street Journal*. In essence, he was promoting the benefits of whole foods and claimed that by eating a healthier diet, many sicknesses and chronic diseases can be prevented. He was outspoken in announcing that the government should not have any part in healthcare reforms. His comments were controversial and upset some people. Whole Foods' experience with social media had been extremely positive in the promotion of their brand and online exposure, but this incident is demonstrating to Whole Foods another side of social media. John McKay's comments spurred some people to form a Facebook group called Boycott Whole Foods. Within a week,

Boycott Whole Foods generated a Facebook following of over 22,000. The Boycott Whole Foods group created a blog, organizes picketing events, and is increasing its Facebook supporters by thousands every day. The group is encouraging people to spend their money elsewhere, and the community members are suggesting alternate health foods resources. This boycott has been totally driven by consumers through social media, and has elicited a public response from Whole Foods, shared via a Facebook note that reads, "First off, whether you agree with John or not, our 50,000+ team members who live and work in your communities will continue to work hard every day to bring you the best natural organic products available. We hope you will continue to give us the opportunity to serve you." Companies can no longer do and say whatever they like without repercussions. This incidence with Whole Foods shows the power that the ordinary person has to take a stand and gain support over unpopular actions of organizations that impact the bottom line.

Would it be wise at this point for John Mackey to make an apology? Everyone is entitled to their own opinion and not everyone is going to agree. He would do well to stand up and engage or talk with his online community by either doing webcasts every now and then to show a different side of him, or at least to start building or rebuilding relationships. To ignore it will just make it grow.

Will it Blend? victory

Blendtec increased its sales dramatically by running the often humorous "Will it Blend" Videos on YouTube, blending everything from an iPhone to a sneaker. Their fans continue to grow exponentially every day, and although this campaign was started several years ago, it is still extremely viral and has traction today. This campaign consists of an ongoing series of infomercials demonstrating the Blendtec line of blenders, especially the Total Blender. In the show, Tom Dickson, the Blendtec founder, attempts to blend various unusual items in order to show off the power of his blender. Dickson started this marketing campaign after doing a blending attempt with a box of matches. At some point during the blending process, a subtitle appears stating whether or not the particular items are safe to blend at home. Golf balls, marbles, cell phones and cubic zirconia, for example, are not safe. These show the subtitle "Don't try this at home." On the other hand, credit cards, ice, and a McDonald's Extra Value Meal® are safe to blend. These show the subtitle "Please try this at home." While the item is being blended, Dickson is smiling and waiting for the process to end. When it does, Dickson frequently warns viewers not to breathe the smoke or dust that results when blending unsafe items by saying, "Don't breathe this!" At the end of each video, the contents are emptied out onto a work top, at which point the subtitle, "Yes, it blends!" appears.

One of the most famous Will it Blend? creations is the "co-chicken," which is half a chicken (cooked, usually rotisserie) blended with 12 fluid ounces of Coca-Cola (without the can). Although the show's example was blended with the bones (and thus was disclaimed as unsafe to eat), a boneless version was made on NBC's *Today* show and served to Meredith Vieira.

Popular fan requests for the show include blending either another blender or a crowbar. It is highly unlikely that either would blend, and this probably means that neither would even be attempted, because of the nature and purpose of the show—marketing Blendtec products. A demonstration video featuring the anticipated crowbar was interrupted by a cell phone call, to which Dickson responds by stuffing the entire crew's cell phones into the blender and blending them, instead. The show has attempted to blend increasingly unlikely items, such as a six foot garden rake and a sealed can of soda.

Lifespan victory

Lifespan used Twitter to proactively reach out to patients and their family and friends who were visiting its hospitals. Their goal was to engage in personal conversation to build loyalty and be aware of what was being said about them, and have that serve as an extension of the strategic marketing plan. More often than not, the comments posted about the hospitals were positive.

Shortly after establishing their Twitter accounts, they started using Twitter's terrific "search" function to look for any mentions of their hospitals. If someone Tweeted that they were "visiting mom at Rhode Island Hospital," for example, they'd Tweet them directly and wish them all the best, in a very personal tone. Keep in mind these "conversations" can be read by thousands of Twitter users. The responses they received to these direct Tweets were amazing. First, the person is surprised that the hospital is actually on Twitter. Second, they express sincere appreciation that they took time to message them back in a personal way.

One of their facilities, Newport Hospital, had an ongoing Twitter conversation with a man whose mother had been in the ICU and finally released. He couldn't thank the hospital enough—not only for the care she received, but also for the concern they expressed on a personal level through these Tweets.

Addressing negative issues can also be accomplished through this new medium. One woman Tweeted that she was late for her appointment because she couldn't find her way around the very large, urban Rhode Island Hospital campus. They responded that indeed, it can be confusing, apologized for the inconvenience, and sent her a link to a campus map on the web, saying she could contact them anytime. Her appreciation was clear in her responses.

United Linen victory

Not all social media success stories come from large, global companies. United Linen, a professional uniform and linen laundry services in Oklahoma, effectively used social media and continues to grow its business and interact with customers. The company leverages a blog on its website to provide customers with posts and videos on everything from ordering linens for major holidays, to the company's winter delivery schedule. United Linen is also extremely active on Twitter, posting several Tweets throughout the day to promote new blog content, ReTweet others' relevant content, and engage with followers. The small B2B company boasts more than 1,600 targeted followers, which can equate to a substantial amount of business and exposure. The company has reported an increase in sales due to their social media efforts.

The power of social media is yet to be grasped by many individuals and businesses around the globe. Hopefully this book brought to light not only the importance of connection online but how you can really utilize social marketing to bring your brand forward and build lifelong, life-changing relationships into your center of influence.

ACKNOWLEDGMENTS

This book would not be in your hands if it wasn't for the amazing team of friends at Entrepreneur Media that believed in me. I cannot thank my editor, Jere Calmes, enough for not only signing me up, but being there for me every step of the way. Thanks go to my online columnist editor, Laura Lorber, and the editor-in-chief of *Entrepreneur* magazine, Amy Cosper, for being just all-around awesome—not just to write for but to hang out and have conversation over yummy dinners and delicious cocktails. To Mike Ludlum, my events coordinator, who always recommends me as the go-to speaker for social media: your confidence and referrals are heartfelt and appreciated more than you know.

Aside from my most amazing publishing team, I am truly grateful for my family for putting up with me during all of the research, sleepless nights rewriting, last minute deadlines, and crazy-idea calls. To my honey, Giles Fabris, thank you for putting food under me when I was in the middle of the "process," and for taking care of my dogs Lucy and Joey so they actually could see the light of day. My kids, Austin, now 21, Savannah, 18 and Jackson, 12: your "go mom" cheers and pep rallies are lifetime memories for me and bring me to tears as I type this. Your constant support and love while I built and continue to build my career is something that is priceless and so deeply appreciated. You are all three the reason behind who I became and am as a person and will continue to become. Your brilliant individual marketing minds, idea factory of concepts, and constant seeking to learn continue to inspire me every moment of the day. I am so proud of my children, so loved by them and love them so much, thank you my loves (I will leave out your nicknames to spare them embarrassment). Oh heck, here goes: Austin: my "M man," Savannah: my "noodle bug," and Jackson: my "love cup." Sorry—it had to be done!

How my mother Heidi Borchers, a best-selling author herself puts up with me, my schedule, my crazy ideas, last minute deadlines, and requests is beyond me; a mother's love as they say. However, my mom's love is beyond that; it is friendship, respect, all around fun and special at every turn. Thank you mom for you are truly my number one fan, I love you.

All my mentors—online and off—I thank you for your constant support, ideas, feedback, and enthusiasm. Michael Port, Mitch Meyerson, Scott Stratten, Gary Vaynerchuk, Dan Schwabel, Jack Canfield, Gay Hendricks, Jane Deuber, John Dulworth, Sprint, Deluxe, Meeting Planners International, Infusionsoft, TalkFusion, Enowit.com, MediaTemple, Jody Jelas my amazing webgal and her team, Kellie and Steve, Kara Clark my graphic design, Pacha, my other amazing graphic designer and Vanessa Sticklin, my best friend and center of support.

To all of my online friends, fans, connections, supporters, bffs: Wow! Every single day engaging with you, listening to you, talking, sharing, is an experience and a moment. I love every interaction (even the ones that are sometimes a bit hard to hear, aka "constructive criticism"). I cherish you, our friendship, and our constant mission and focus to make this world a better, safer, healthier place to enjoy. If I named every single person that I love online, this book would be 1,000 pages long, so please know that if I am connected to you online, there is a reason for it, as I do not just reach out or accept invites from just anyone. It is because you are you and I felt or saw something that I liked or wanted to get to know more about that we are connected. Thank you all for your awesomeness and for buying this book as well as sharing it with the world. Your love and support moves me every day to do more, be more and act more.

I am truly grateful to Facebook, Twitter, LinkedIn, and YouTube for bringing these people into my life and making it even more beautiful. To all of the brains behind the development, launch, and ongoing success of these platforms (too many names to mention), thank you for standing up for your dream, taking action, and moving through adversity, doubt, and obstacles. You are an inspiration to me and I truly appreciate all that you have brought to this world and into my life.

ABOUT THE AUTHOR

Starr Hall is a publicist and social media strategist who serves clients worldwide. Achieving success at a relatively young age, she left a VP of PR position at a high-powered corporate advertising agency to start her own marketing agency, 2 Point Media. Beginning with just two clients, within two years she had acquired more than 70 active clients from around the globe before selling the company to a national firm. Starr has grown her personal business 423 percent through social networking in the last nine months alone!

Starr has established effective relationships with over 1,200 editors and broadcast producers worldwide, and has secured mass coverage and media placement for her clients in regional, national, and international newspapers, magazines, radio, television, and internet outlets such as *Good Morning America*, *The Today Show*, *Oprah* magazine, *Entrepreneur* magazine, *Inc.* magazine, *The Wall Street Journal*, *Los Angeles Times*, *DIY,* and *HGTV*. She has also secured major book contracts and co-branding deals for clients with Time Warner Publishing, Entrepreneur Press, F+W Publications, and Wiley and Sons, the publisher of the *For Dummies* series.

She is the social media columnist for *Entrepreneur* magazine online and a regularly featured columnist for *American Express Small Business Open Forum*. Her previous book with Entrepreneur Press is *Get Connected: The Social Networking Toolkit for Business* and is available wherever books are sold.

Keep updated on Twitter with the hashtag for this book, #socialwavebook, on the Facebook page facebook.com/starrhalldotcom, or at the site for this book, socialwavebook.com.

INDEX